Generations

This script is published by
DCG Publications.

All inquiries regarding purchase of further scripts and current royalty rates should be addressed to:

DCG Media Group
Vamos 73008
Chania
Crete
Greece

Email: info@dcgmediagroup.com
www.dcgmediagroup.com

Conditions

- ❖ All DCG Publication scripts are fully protected by the copyright acts. Under no circumstances must they be reproduced by photo-copying or any other means, either in whole or in part.

- ❖ The license to perform referred to above only relates to live performances of this script. A separate license is required for video-taping or sound recording, which will be issued on receipt of the appropriate fee.

- ❖ The name of the author shall be clearly stated on all publicity, programs etc. The program credits shall state "Script provided by DCG Publications".

Generations
By
Glyn Jones

DCG
Publications

First Published in Greece 2010

© Glyn Jones

The author's moral rights have been asserted

DCG Publications
www.dcgmediagroup.com

ISBN 978-960-98418-9-4

Typeset by
DCG Publications

Printed in England by
Lightning Source.

First Produced
at the
James Madison University Experimental Theatre
Wampler
28th Sept - 2nd Oct 1986

Directed by
Edward Christian Holloway

Set design
Joel Mathew Morritz

Cast List
In order of appearance

Bessie	Janice O'Rourke
Laura	Virginia Hamilton
Sharon	Jennifer Rayfield
Lindy	Tracy Y. Lee

The scene is a kitchen/living room
of a dilapidated house on route 33
Virginia USA

Generations was selected for the
Carnegie Mellon Drama
Showcase of New Plays 1991

The house on Route 33 which inspired the play

ACT ONE

The live-in kitchen and, beyond it, the veranda of a large old wooden house just off Route 33, Virginia. The house is set on the side of a hill so that the landscape beyond the veranda is not seen. Even if it could be, it would, at the moment, be mostly obscured by washing hanging on the veranda to dry.
The furniture is sparse, old, and poor yard sale junk.
One door leads from the kitchen to the rest of the house.
It is mid afternoon, an unseasonably warm afternoon for the time of year.
Silence - and then, from offstage, a loud yell. It is BESSIE who is in the yard below the veranda.

BESSIE: GODDAMMIT!

The yell is followed by a very loud bang as a rock, hurled with full strength, hits something like an old iron bath tub.

    I'll kill it! Kill it! I'll kill it!

A couple of cans are kicked out of the way, followed by the sound of feet ascending the wooden stairs, and BESSIE passes by outside a window, disappears behind the wall, and reappears at the open door. She practically wrenches the screen door off its hinges and rampages across the room.

    Goddammit! Squattin' there with its tail up like a goddam squirrel. Well it's done it for the last time, the last time. That is the very last time!

She disappears through the inner door and, after a moment, reappears holding a shotgun, crossing back the way she came.

    Pissed all over it! All over it! Squattin'. Squattin' there with its fur all quiverin'... Sprayin' like a goddam burst pipe... jus' sittin' there, starin' at me as I come round the corner. Quiverin'!

She kicks open the screen door and goes back along the veranda, addressing an unseen body as she goes.

>   Didn't you see it?

BESSIE disappears, clomping down the veranda stairs.

LAURA appears at the inner door. She has been resting and is dressed only in a slip over which she has pulled a too big, holey cardigan which she holds wrapped around herself. LAURA is twenty-four, very pretty. Still in the process of waking up, she leans against the doorjamb for a moment.

LAURA: What's goin' on out there?

She moves into the room, crosses to the table, picks up a pack of cigarettes and a lighter. She is about to light the cigarette when... SHOTGUN BLAST.

Laura screams, drops the cigarette and lighter, and heads cautiously for the veranda door.

>   Who's shootin'? Who's out there? (*She stops at the screen door and looks out.*) What's goin' on out there? (*She looks along the veranda.*) Gran'ma? What's goin' on? (*There being nothing obviously threatening, she pushes open the screen and goes out onto the veranda, pushes aside some of the washing and looks over the rail.*) Ma? Is that you?

BESSIE: Who the hell you think it is?

LAURA: What you shootin' at?

BESSIE: Cat.

LAURA: Ya get it?

BESSIE: No. Leastways not dead.

LAURA: Oh. (*She watches.*) Where'd it go?

BESSIE: Skud off behind the barn. Got buckshot up its ass I reckon. Hell, you should ha' seen it go!

LAURA: Why you shootin' at it anyway?

BESSIE: I told you about that! Sprayin' everywhere. Now it's gone an' pissed all over my clean washin'. Dirty sonofabitch! Where'd it come from? That's what I'd like to know. An' she sat there the whole time watchin' it an' never said a word.

LAURA turns to look at the person seated against the wall beside the door.

LAURA: Gran'ma? Did you see it? *(Turns back.)* She didn't see it. How'd you expect her to see it with all this hangin' up here? *(She indicates the washing.)*

SHOTGUN BLAST. LAURA screams. BESSIE yells in triumph.

BESSIE: Yahoo!

LAURA: Did you get it?

BESSIE: No. Got somethin' else though.

LAURA: What?

BESSIE: Got that darned possum outa the woodpile.

LAURA backs away towards the door, opens the screen and stands behind it, keeping her eye on the stairs.

Stuck his nose out to see what was goin' on I reckon.

LAURA: Don't bring it up here! Don't!

BESSIE, carrying the gun and the remains of the blasted possum, passes the window. LAURA screams, dashes inside, slamming the screen door behind her. She looks out through the window.

BESSIE: Got more'n he bargained for. *(She holds out the possum to the body behind the wall.)* Here... you

	want it?
LAURA:	Don't do that, mama. Don't do that!
BESSIE:	Can't see a goddam cat pissin' on my washin'...
LAURA:	You're scarin' her. Don't do that!
BESSIE:	...maybe you can see what's right under your nose.
LAURA:	You're getting blood all over her! Don't do that!
BESSIE:	Oh, quit your yellin'. She don't even know what's happenin'. What good is she anyway? Blind. Deaf, dumb, an' blind. Reckon she can't smell neither. If she could she'd just die from smellin' her own stink.

She turns away and hurls the remains of the possum over the veranda rail.

LAURA:	Mama! What you doin' that for?
BESSIE:	What dya want me to do?
LAURA:	You just gonna leave it lyin' out there in the yard? It'll stink. It'll lie out there an' rot an' stink.
BESSIE:	If'n it had died natural in the woodpile it would stink wouldn't it?
LAURA:	That's no reason.
BESSIE:	*(Re-entering the house.)* If you don't like it you go move it.
LAURA:	It'll bring disease.
BESSIE:	Huh! Listen who's talkin'! She's got three kids covered in ringworm an' she talks disease.
LAURA:	It's your dogs gave 'em the ringworm. Those dogs

	ought to be put down.
BESSIE:	Don't tell me how to run my house, girl. You're livin' here under sufferance you know, that's what you're livin' under.
LAURA:	What do you mean? I'm your daughter.
BESSIE:	Huh! Anyway, the dogs that ought to be put down will get the possum an' then it won't stink no more. 'Cept as dogshit. Ha ha ha! That's the trouble with this old world if you want to know. Too much shit. Too much piss. An' she pisses more'n anybody.
LAURA:	She's old.
BESSIE:	I know she's old. I don't have to be told she's old.
LAURA:	It's not her fault she can't control herself no more.

BESSIE stands the gun upright in a corner.

	You ain't leavin' that gun there!
BESSIE:	*(Glaring at her.)* An' why the hell not?
LAURA:	It ain't safe, that's why the hell not. Leavin' guns standin' in corners.

She picks up her cigarette and lights it, taking a short, sharp puff, and sniffing loudly.

BESSIE:	Look, girl, stead of standin' there smokin' yourself to death, why don'tcha go get some clothes on an' start doin' somethin' useful round here?

She goes to the sink and starts washing the blood from her hands.

LAURA:	I wouldn't feel safe with that gun standin' there. It could fall and go off... both barrels!
BESSIE:	Get some clothes on an' when it blasts the hell outa

	you you'll at least look respectable.
LAURA:	*(Pleading.)* Mama!
BESSIE:	Shee-it! Now do like I say! It ain't decent, walkin' round the house naked.
LAURA:	What do you mean? Naked! *(She pulls the cardigan tighter around her.)* An' who's to see me anyway?
BESSIE:	*(Reaches for a towel and wipes her hands.)* Lyin' around all day.
LAURA:	I hate this place.
BESSIE:	Then what're you doin' here?
LAURA:	Got nowhere to go.
BESSIE:	Get some damn fool man to take you in.
LAURA:	Not with kids. I gotta think of the kids.
BESSIE:	It's no wonder that husband of yourn threw you out.
LAURA:	He did no such thing.
BESSIE:	And what did he throw you out of? *(Laughing)* A trashed trailer...
LAURA:	Mobile home.
BESSIE:	Mobile all right. You can take it to the dump in a hand basket. Older than me. Older'n her out there... *(pointing to the veranda)* ...an' about as much use. An' what's worse, he don' even own it.
LAURA:	*(Heading for the door.)* Under no circumstances do I wish to discuss my ex-husband.
BESSIE:	He ain't your ex-husband. Not yet awhile.

LAURA: I'm suing for divorce aren't I?

BESSIE: *(Throwing away the towel.)* Suing's one thing, gettin's another. Anyway, I thought you didn't want to discuss it.

With another sniff LAURA turns and leaves the room. BESSIE watches her go. Shakes her head.

A great Thanksgiving this is going to be. *(She opens the screen door and looks out.)* Don't have to worry 'bout the dogs tonight but reckon you'll want feedin'. Don't know why. Throwing away good food I call it. She don't taste it. Don't do her no good. Food is for nurturing. How you supposed to nurture a skeleton? Why don't she just die? Why don't you just die? Huh? Can you hear me? Look at you. You're all skin and bones. Do you hear what I'm telling you? Why don't you just die? Get your old bones off my old bones.

LAURA reappears at the inner door. She has slipped on an old faded cotton dress.

LAURA: Why don't you just leave her alone?

BESSIE: *(Turning back into the room.)* Is that what you call dressed?

LAURA: You should leave her alone.

BESSIE: *(Moving to a cupboard.)* Wish that I could. *(She takes down a large can from the cupboard and places it on the table. Takes off the lid.)*

LAURA: You making corn bread?

BESSIE: *(Gives LAURA a withering look.)* It's Thanksgiving, ain't it? Though you tell me what I got to be thankful for. And I'm baking pumpkin pie. AND sweet potatoes. I'm as American as anybody. Any

	more questions?
LAURA:	Where'd you get the money for the turkey?
BESSIE:	None of your business.
LAURA:	Where'd you get it?
BESSIE:	Whatsa matter with you? You gone deaf?
LAURA:	Where'd you get it?
BESSIE:	Traded for it.
LAURA:	Traded what?
BESSIE:	None of your business. Any more questions?
LAURA:	You been in my jewellery box?
BESSIE:	Jewellery box! Jewellery box! What jewellery box?
LAURA:	My Japan box. The one made from pressed paper, with the mountain on it. It's got my rhinestone in it. Unless you took it.
BESSIE:	Lady, your rhinestone ain't worth a pig's fart.
LAURA:	It is too! Don't say that. It was the best thing Ray ever give me.
BESSIE:	*(Carrying on her preparations for the meal.)* I told you all along not to marry that boy. How come kids never listen? Why you had to go marry a boy ain't got a pot to piss in or a window to throw it out of sure beats the hell out of me.
LAURA:	What about his bike?
BESSIE:	What about it? Can't even keep up his payments. It's gonna be took from him.

LAURA:		He'll keep them up. He won't lose that bike.
BESSIE:		Sure. He can lose his wife, lose his kids, but he'll die before he loses his bike.
LAURA:		It's not Ray's fault he can't get a job. Job's is scarce.
BESSIE:		He can't find a job because he don't want a job.
LAURA:		Not true.
BESSIE:		A handful of "gimmes" and a mouth full of "much obligeds" that's Ray Peterson, just like the rest of that family. The only time your man's alive is when he's beating the shit outa you and the kids. When he's on his bike trashing the highway with empty sixpacks. An' one of these days he's gonna trash it with corpses including, I hope, his own. What's that man ever give you, apart from your precious rhinestone, but a hard time and three snotty brats?
LAURA:		My kids are good kids.
BESSIE:		Bullshit! They white trash, just like their daddy. *(Shouting out the window.)* You hear that? Your great-grandchildren are trash! Eighty-eight years old an' all you got to show for it is trash. Well never you mind. You'll get your just rewards in that heaven you was always preachin' about.
LAURA:		An' you're gonna go to hell, the way you treat her, your own mother.
BESSIE:		She ain't my mother. Leastways not since I was nine years old.
LAURA:		What are you talking about? She's your mother! How would you like it if your children...?
BESSIE:		I don't want to talk about it. Like you don't want to discuss your husband. Are you gonna help me here or not? *(She hands LAURA a bowl of eggs.)* Here..

beat these. You do know how to do it I suppose. And wash your hands first... please.

LAURA takes the bowl over to the sink and turns on the water. She stands for a moment looking down.

LAURA: There's blood in this sink.

BESSIE: Then wash it out.

LAURA: *(Silence for a moment as she does it.)* Couldn't ever get used to blood.

BESSIE: You grew up on a farm and you can't get used to blood?

LAURA: Never will.

BESSIE: What happens when one of your kids gets cut?

LAURA: That's different.

BESSIE: How? Different.

LAURA: I love my kids.

BESSIE: Huh! Why don't you look after them then? Couldn't even go to school. All the other parents objected. Formed a committee. Got up a petition. Said if the Peterson kids were gonna keep on goin' to school then their kids weren't. An' what did the health man say? Get 'em treated or else. An' what did their father do? Shaved their heads an' took 'em back. Took 'em back with shaved heads. How do you think they felt about that?

LAURA: It's not Ray's fault. He comes from a bad family.

BESSIE: That's what I said.

LAURA: I heard you! I heard you! I heard you a million times! Now shut up about it!

BESSIE ignores this outburst and calmly carries on with what she is doing.

        And, if you want to know, I only married him to get away from you.

BESSIE: You married him because you were stupid.

Silence.

LAURA: He didn't beat the kids. He never beat them, not once. I only said he did because I was mad at him. He never beat me.

BESSIE: I got eyes in my head. And ears. You think I'm like her out there?

Silence.

LAURA: Sure is warm for this time of year.

BESSIE: Your sister's late.

LAURA: You want me to bring in the washing? Should be dry by now.

She goes out to collect the washing but stops by the door and bends down.

        Gran? You all right? You need a drink? I think she needs a drink.

BESSIE: Then give her a drink. What's stopping you?

LAURA re-enters the room and crosses to the stove, looks inside an old-fashioned coffee pot sitting there.

LAURA: You want a cup of coffee? I can heat this up. Should be okay.

BESSIE: What's the matter with you, girl? It's first one

thing then another. I thought you was bringing in the washing.

LAURA: *(She has switched on the stove beneath the coffee pot and now walks over to the sink.)* I'll give gran a drink then I'll bring it in.

LAURA rinses out an enamel drinking mug with a spout and fills it with water. She takes it outside.

BESSIE: An', if you see that cat, kill it. Maybe you can't kill it. Maybe he's got the devil inside him, that cat. You can see it in his eyes, the mean way he looks at you. You can see it the way he's all beat up. Well the devil's got buckshot up his tail now, see how he likes that.

LAURA: *(Coming back in with some washing.)* You didn't even hit him. He wouldn't have run off if'n you'd hit him.

BESSIE: I must ha' hit him. That close?

LAURA: Cats is small.

BESSIE: Not this one. This one's the biggest ugliest cat I ever seen.

LAURA: *(Starts to fold the washing.)* That close the shot didn't even scatter. Probably went right over his head. Maybe you hit the barn but you never hit that cat. Bet you the side of the barn's all over peppered with buckshot. Time it were pulled down anyway. Full of wood borer.

BESSIE: Whatsa matter with you Laura May Peterson? You're spoutin' a whole lot of opinion round here. You want my dogs put down. Now you want my barn burnt down. There ain't much left round here but I'm the one who says what goes and when it goes, and that includes you.

LAURA: You want a cup of coffee?

BESSIE: *(Shakes her head, sits at the table and looks around the room.)* I was born in this house. I brought your daddy back to this house after we were married. I think I'm gonna die in this house. Why not? Everyone dies in this house. Or they come back to be buried here. *(Indicating the veranda.)* She come back. This house isn't just a house. It's the people who were born in it, raised in it, lived in it. You, growing up the wild thing you were, payin' no heed to nobody...Your sister Sharon... my sister, Dorcus. When I heard Dorcus had died... I brung her back... all the way from Tennessee. She was so good. So pretty and so good. They say the good die young. Is that what they say? I don't know what it's all about. These days I reckon there's nobody knows what it's all about. Some say this, some say that. I don't know anymore if there's a heaven or if there's a hell. I used to know. When I was a little girl. I believed then. Now I don't know. But, if there is a heaven, then that's where my sister is. And, if there are angels, then that's what my sister is, one of God's brightest angels, sitting on his right hand. These days there's folks even say the Bible ain't true. An' there's those say every word is true but all they talk about is cancer an' if you give five bucks to the Lord he'll save you. Dorcus believed. It didn't save her. I brought her back from Tennessee, buried her here. Paid for the casket, paid to bring her back, paid for the burial. I took all my savings and what was left I gave to the church in memory of her. She would have liked that. It was the least I could do. I couldn't do anything for her in her lifetime, wasn't in no position to. Couldn't thank her for all she did for me. But I made it up to her. I made it up. Wherever she is, I hope she knows that I loved her.

LAURA: She knows, mama. She knows.

BESSIE: *(Rising.)* This ain't gettin' the dinner ready.

	(Looking hard at her daughter.) You ain't never visited her grave.
LAURA:	I will if you want me to.
BESSIE:	*(Stands for a moment and then shrugs.)* What does it matter?

She goes back to her work. LAURA starts to fold the laundry.

LAURA:	I bet you was pretty. *(No response.)* When you were a girl. *(No response.)* I bet you were the prettiest girl for miles. *(No response.)* You still are, you know that?

BESSIE laughs.

LAURA:	Sharon's pretty too. No, she's beautiful, really beautiful. In fact we're a family of good-lookers, you know that? The best in these parts anyway.
BESSIE:	Pride comes before a fall, my girl, watch your tongue. What'd being pretty ever get us anyway except a whole heap of trouble? What'd it get you? Pregnant at fourteen, a child bride, married to a man who hasn't got the brains nor manners of a hog. In fact, next to Ray Peterson, the hog is a perfect gentleman.
LAURA:	You never liked him.
BESSIE:	Course I never liked him. Never liked any of that family. Give me one reason why I oughter like him.
LAURA:	Maybe if you'd tried we wouldn't have fought so much.
BESSIE:	I'm the reason for the fightin'? You're blamin' me?
LAURA:	That was the reason sometimes.

BESSIE: He badmouthed me an' you stood up to him, that was the reason.

LAURA: He only badmouthed you because he knew you were badmouthin' him.

BESSIE: What did he say about me?

LAURA: Who cares? It's over now.

BESSIE: No, it's not over, and I care. You're still his wife.

LAURA: I'm getting a divorce.

BESSIE: You're the mother of his three kids. At least I think you are. Are you?

LAURA: You can say some real dirty things sometimes, you know that?

BESSIE: It's a dirty world full of dirty people. Are they all his?

LAURA: Don't they look like they're all his?

BESSIE: Yes, they got his dirty good looks all right. I don't deny his good looks. That's where all the trouble started. You were unlucky, my girl. You're the one got caught. Three kids. What're you going to do, Laura?

LAURA: What?

BESSIE: What do you mean, what? What's what supposed to mean? What are you going to do? That's what!

LAURA: Get a job I guess.

BESSIE: Yes? And what do you think you're gonna do? And who's gonna look after the children while you're at work? And what kind of work would you get anyway? You ain't fit for nothing, girl.

LAURA: I could get training.

BESSIE: At what?

LAURA: I don't know. MacDonald's or something. I could clean kitchen.

BESSIE: You wouldn't last a week.

LAURA: Well okay then, you make a suggestion, seein' as to how you're so smart.

BESSIE: Get married again.

LAURA: What!

BESSIE: You got yourself an' three kids to keep an' you're not capable. Find someone who is. Only this time... this time try to find a man who's different.

LAURA: How do you mean, different?

BESSIE: Find a man who when he stands next to a hog you know who is the man and who is the hog.

LAURA laughs.

What's so funny?

LAURA shakes her head.

You don't even know what I'm talking about and you think it's funny.

LAURA: I'll bring in the washing.

BESSIE: Does that mean we've stopped talking?

LAURA: No. You can talk all you want. But that's all it is. How many men you know gonna take on a woman already got three kids? Might be different if the

	kids were growed.
BESSIE:	You tried it once, marryin' for love, and it didn't work out. Happens all the time. Maybe if you hadn't been pregnant... well now's the time to try it again, with your eyes wide open, knowin' what you're walkin' into. Use some sense. Try to do somethin' with your life.
LAURA:	Look, mama... I need some time. I been married to Ray for nigh on ten years. I'm not even divorced yet. We're seperated, is all. Not divorced.
BESSIE:	You're thinking of going back to him!
LAURA:	*(Shakes her head.)* No. Sometimes I want to. I think about it. But I couldn't. Not after all that. I lie in bed at night and I think about him. I wake up in the morning and I think about him. I can see him so clear, feel him, smell him. We make love. We talk. It's beautiful I want to cry. I cry my tears into his hand. I hold his open hand to my mouth and I cry my tears into it. Then I feel him squeeze my chin, and he squeezes harder, and harder. And suddenly I'm scared. I'm real scared of him, mama. You never seen him when he gets real mad. You don't know what he can do. He cracked three of my ribs once. You didn't know that did you? I couldn't breathe. I thought I was going to die. Threw me against the table, corner of the table, threw me right across the room. And, when Ray Junior tried to stop him, yellin' an' screamin' an' cryin', "Daddy, don't! Don't, daddy! Please, daddy!" he just picked up that kid an' threw him right across the room too. Could have killed him. If Ray Junior's head'd hit something hard, or sharp, could have killed him. And when I tried to protect my baby, coverin' him with my body, he kicked me. Went on kicking. And you say I don't love my kids? Why you think I've got them over to Lindy Johnson's house? Because he's gonna come lookin' for them. He's had time on his own now. He's been

	thinking. Sitting there in that trailer, thinking, 'bout me and the kids, about how he's not gettin' it, 'bout how he really loves me and how he wants me back. And, even if he doesn't want me, he's gonna want his kids an' he's gonna come lookin' for 'em. And I know Ray... to-day's the day. He'll come over here and he'll say, "Happy Thanksgiving," but what he's really come for are his boys and who knows what he'll do to get them? That's why I took them over to Lindy's. He won't think to look there, not in a black house. He doesn't even know we're friends. I never told him. He'd have jest got mad. Yes, mama, if I thought he'd change, I'd go back to him. But he scares me.
BESSIE:	Then do what I say, find a man who'll treat you right, someone who'll look after the kids, love 'em, bring 'em up right. Teach them to be gentle so they'll be different. Then things'll start to change maybe. Then maybe folk can feel pleased to be pretty, and not scared.
LAURA:	You got someone in mind haven't you?
BESSIE:	*(Nods.)* Aaron Williams.
LAURA:	Aaron! *(She shrieks with laughter.)* Aaron Williams! Aaron Williams is forty years old an' lives with his mother.
BESSIE:	You'll be forty years old and still livin' with your mother but not if I can help it.
LAURA:	Aaron Williams... he looks like a turtle's lost his shell.
BESSIE:	Is that all you can think about? What a man looks like?
LAURA:	Aaron ain't never looked at a girl in his whole life.
BESSIE:	Maybe that's because the girls are all like you an'

	don't look at him. Can't see beyond their own silly noses. Anyway, how do you know he ain't ever looked at a girl? You been around him all your life?
LAURA:	It's what everybody says.
BESSIE:	What everybody says! Everybody's always sayin'. Sayin' this, sayin' that. Seems to me nobody lives their own lives, everybody else is too busy livin' it for them.
LAURA:	*(Chuckling.)* Aaron Williams... I don't even know if he can talk. I never heard him talk. He never opens his mouth. He just nods.
BESSIE:	He talks.
LAURA:	You've talked with him?
BESSIE:	Sure. I see him in town and we talk. We've talked a lot. And he's got a lot to say when you get him going. He's a very interesting man.
LAURA:	Well, if he's so interesting, you marry him.
BESSIE:	I could do a whole lot worse.
LAURA:	I don't believe this. I suppose you talked some about me.
BESSIE:	You came into the conversation.
LAURA:	Oh, I came into the conversation. How's that?
BESSIE:	'Cause he always asks after you, that's how. So don't tell me Aaron ain't ever looked at a girl because he's looked at you.
LAURA:	*(Not sure of what to say to this.)* Well... that's creepy.
BESSIE:	And I know he thinks fondly of you.

LAURA smiles.

BESSIE: Don't laugh at him, Laura, no matter what you think of him.

LAURA: It's not just what I think of him. It's what the whole town thinks of him. And they wouldn't just be laughing at him. They'd be laughing at me.

BESSIE: Feelings ain't to be laughed at. Could be he's too good for you.

LAURA: Oh, thanks a lot!

BESSIE: Well, at least think about it.

LAURA: Nothing to think about. Can you imagine Aaron with no clothes on? Can you imagine his feet? I bet he's got toes like a frog. Can you imagine his... THING? *(Peals of laughter.)* Can you imagine Aaron DOIN' it? Oh dear... Oh, dear God! *(She wipes away her tears with a corner of washing.)*

BESSIE has ignored it all, carries on with what she is doing.

You're crazy, you know that? Crazy! I'd die laughing, mama. I'd shit Twinkies! *(The laughter subsides as she gradually recovers, looks at her mother.)* Well? Haven't you anything to say?

BESSIE: What's to say? You've said it all. Maybe I was wrong.

LAURA: You sure were.

BESSIE: Wrong to wish YOU on HIM. I'm wonderin' if you should be wished on to anybody. I'm wonderin' if it was all Ray's fault he beat you up.

LAURA: I didn't do anything!

BESSIE: Who knows?

LAURA: What makes you say that?

BESSIE: Because I wasn't born yesterday and because you got that look on your face you always had when you was little and tryin' to hide somethin'.

LAURA: Mama, I got to get away from here! I can't do anything here! I got to go where people don't know me, where Ray can't get at me.

BESSIE: When you get your divorce he'll leave you alone. He don't dare touch you then.

LAURA: Are you kidding?

BESSIE: Where you proposing to go anyway?

LAURA: *(Hardly audible.)* Philadelphia.

BESSIE: *(Who heard it anyway.)* What did you say?

LAURA: Philadelphia.

BESSIE: *(Recovering from the shock.)* What in the hell do you want to go to Philadelphia for?

LAURA: There's a friend of Lindy's lives there. She says I can stay with her an' she can find me a job.

BESSIE: *(Vehemently.)* You're lyin', Laura May!

LAURA: I'm not lyin', mama, I swear it!

BESSIE: You been doin' somethin' dirty and you're scared of bein' found out and you're runnin' away, just like you did when you were a little girl. You were screwin' around with boys before you even had tits. You knew what a pecker looked like before it had hair round it. I knew it. I always knew it. And every time I knew it you tried to run away before I switched you for it. And you're wantin' to run away again. Well you can't do it, Laura May. Comes a time you gotta stop runnin' away, because you're runnin' from yourself and there ain't no place to go.

LAURA: And you whipped me good, didn't you, mama? You whipped me real good. I can remember. I can remember the hurt, the screamin', the blood on my legs. You talk about love, you talk about changin' things, about runnin' away. What were you runnin' from, mama? Why did you have to take it out on me?

BESSIE: It was for your own good. Do you think I liked whipping you? Think I enjoyed it?

LAURA: Maybe I fooled around with boys because I was lookin' for somethin' I couldn't get in this house. Have you thought of that?

For a long moment mother and daughter stand facing each other, then BESSIE turns away.

BESSIE: So you're plannin' on goin' to Philadelphia. You think jobs is goin' to be easier to find up there?

LAURA: I'll find out, won't I?

BESSIE: Philadelphia, huh! An' you ain't never been to a town bigger'n Harrisonburg.

LAURA: So? Won't be that different. Bigger, that's all.

BESSIE: Bigger, an' harder, an' dirtier.

LAURA: How do you know what it's like? You been there?

BESSIE: Don't have to stick my nose in it to know what it is.

LAURA: Well I seen pictures too. There's skyscrapers. Beautiful tall buildings like in New York.

BESSIE: You want to go to New York?

The tone in her voice implies going from Sodom to Gomorrah.

LAURA: Reckon I might just do that. It's not that far away. I can take the Greyhound, or Amtrak. Amtrak goes from Philadelphia to New York, goes from Washington, goes from Charlottesville.

BESSIE: I happen to know where Amtrak goes to and it don't go to heaven. You don't take no train to heaven, my girl. You just take it from one big, dirty, ugly city to the next. What're you going to do in Philadelphia 'cept get yourself into a whole heap of trouble? Who' this friend of Lindy Johnson's? She a colored girl?

LAURA: Yes.

BESSIE: You won't last a week.

LAURA: Mama!

BESSIE: I ain't bringing you back. You get yourself killed in Philadelphia you stay there.

LAURA: Why should I be killed?

BESSIE: Livin' in a colored house in a colored neighborhood? Drugs, stabbings, rapes, muggings, people bein' murdered all the time. Even the police is afraid to go in there. What do you think those niggers is going to do to a pretty white girl? You think they're goin' to leave you alone? You walk down the street there, they ain't just gonna say, "Hiya, Laura, how ya doin'?" They's gonna find out how you doin'?

LAURA: I'll be all right. I'll be with friends.

BESSIE: What's her name? This friend of Lindy Johnson's?

LAURA:	*(Taken by surprise and trying to recover.)* I don't know.
BESSIE:	You don't know?
LAURA:	I don't remember.
BESSIE:	See? I knew you was lyin'.
LAURA:	Lindy mentioned her name but I don't remember.
BESSIE:	How many times she mention it?
LAURA:	I don't know! When we was talking. You expect me to count?
BESSIE:	I expect you to remember the name of someone you're gonna go stay with. If the woman's your way out, if she's gonna be your salvation, you'd remember her name. You don't forget something like that.
LAURA:	Janice! Her name is Janice.
BESSIE:	Janice who?
LAURA:	Oh, for Christ's sake! Lindy's the one who's fixin' it. If you don't believe me, ask her. Go on, ask her. Ask her about her friend Janice.
BESSIE:	The one you're goin' to stay with in Philadelphia.
LAURA:	Yes, the one I'm going to stay with in Philadelphia.
BESSIE:	Lies, all lies.
LAURA:	Shit!

LAURA storms out onto the veranda. BESSIE does not move. There is a moment of silence.

	There's a car coming.
BESSIE:	*(Suddenly she seems older, more tired.)* That'll be Sharon.
LAURA:	*(Waving.)* Yep. It's her.
BESSIE:	Glen with her?
LAURA:	Nope. She's on her own.

The dogs have started to bark. BESSIE picks up the folded laundry and goes into the house with it. LAURA, on the veranda, waves again.

Hi! How ya doin'? Hey, dogs! Quit that! Get down! You hear me? Get down! Kick 'em, Sharon, kick 'em. An' don't touch them. They got ringworm.

BESSIE returns as SHARON passes the window.

SHARON:	Hello, gran'ma. How you doin'?

Outside the door SHARON and LAURA hug each other in greeting.

LAURA:	Oh, it's so good to see you!

They enter the kitchen.

SHARON:	Hello, ma. Sorry I'm late. Was waiting on Glen and he got back only an hour ago.

BESSIE nods, accepting the kiss on the cheek. SHARON is older than her sister by three or four years: taller, an air of quiet easy-going strength about her.

LAURA heads straight for the stove, a new quickness in her movements.

LAURA:	You want coffee? I'll make fresh.

SHARON: Sooner have a drink.

LAURA: Bourbon?

SHARON: Huh-huh.

LAURA switches direction, gets the bottle from a cupboard, and one glass.

You not having one?

LAURA: No. Don't feel like it right now. *(She starts to fix the drink.)* Ma, you want a drink?

BESSIE shakes her head. SHARON sits at the table.

SHARON: So how's everything been with you, ma?

BESSIE: Your sister wants to go to Philadelphia.

SHARON: Oh, really? That's nice. What for?

BESSIE: Says she's going to stay with a friend of Lindy Johnson's. What was her name?

LAURA: Janice.

BESSIE: Janice. Says she's goin' to get a job.

SHARON: Well good luck to her.

BESSIE: That's all you got to say?

SHARON: What do you want? I should wish her bad luck?

BESSIE: I want you to speak to her. She always listened to you.

SHARON: She's never listened to me.

BESSIE: Tell her not to go.

SHARON:	Why? If she wants to go, let her go. It's not for me to tell her what to do. She's a grown woman.
BESSIE:	*(Moving away.)* One as bad as the other.
SHARON:	She can make up her own mind.

LAURA hands SHARON her drink. SHARON follows BESSIE.

	Aw, come on, ma... *(Singing)*..."When I was single, I went dressed so fine, Now I am married, go ragged all the time, Lord, I wish I was a single girl again."
BESSIE:	*(Together.)* Lord, I wish I was a single girl again.
ALL 3:	"When I was single, marryin' was my crave. Now I am married, I'm troubled to my grave. Lord, I wish I was a single girl again."
SHARON:	*(Raising her glass.)* Happy Thanksgiving. *(They are all laughing.)* I got a present for you. It's in the car. *(To LAURA.)* For you too. An' gran. Forgot to bring 'em in.
BESSIE:	You still drivin' that ole Chevvy?
SHARON:	No, ma. I woke up this morning, went out to feed the chickens and, guess what? Somebody had come in the night and delivered a brand new Cadillac right to my front door. There it was... all gleaming... Virginia plates reading my name, decals, key in the ignition, full tank, stereo eight track, fur covered reclin' seats, sun roof. Just waitin' for me to get in an' drive away.
BESSIE:	That crazy old car. You gonna kill yourself in that rattletrap one day. It's gonna run you right off the road and you'll be killed. Then I'll have lost both my daughters.
SHARON:	*(Smiling at LAURA.)* You've lost one already?

BESSIE: Might as well have. Time Glen got you a new car. How old's that car now anyway?

SHARON: Lost count. But it'll do a few miles yet.

LAURA: So how is Glen?

SHARON: Asleep.

BESSIE: Why'nt he come over an' say hello?

SHARON: Because he's alseep.

LAURA: Did he have any luck?

SHARON: Nope. He came in the house and I asked him, "Did you get anything?" "Nope," he said. Then he ate. Then he opened a beer, sat down in front of the tv to watch the game. Then he fell asleep and that's where I left him.

LAURA: That's all he said in all that time? Just "Nope"?

SHARON: My man's a man of few words, the fewer the better.

BESSIE: And he didn't get anything.

SHARON: Nope. Didn't even see anything. Warren Marshall got two. Says, if Glen don't have any better luck, he'll give us a leg. I'll let you have some.

BESSIE: Don't like venison. Never have.

LAURA: Glen goin' out again?

SHARON: Soon as he wakes up. You want a hand over there, ma?

BESSIE: *(At the sink.)* I can manage. You sit there an' talk to your sister.

SHARON: So how you keepin', sister?

LAURA: *(Shrugs.)* Okay.

SHARON: Where the kids?

BESSIE: She took them over to Lindy Johnson's.

LAURA: *(Glaring furiously at her mother.)* I took them over to Lindy Johnson's.

SHARON: Oh? Why's that?

BESSIE: Thinks Ray's gonna come lookin' for 'em.

LAURA: Mother! I got a tongue in my head you know. I thought how Sharon an' me was gonna talk.

BESSIE: Now she's sayin' how she's going to Philadelphia. But she don't make no mention of the kids. Suppose she reckons on leavin' them with me. If Ray comes lookin' for them after she's gone he'll take them away an' hide them someplace. Then she'll lose them for good. But maybe that's what she wants. Well I ain't gonna be responsible.

LAURA: Where's he gonna take them?

BESSIE: To his folks. An' you won't get 'em back, I can promise you that.

LAURA: He won't come lookin' if everybody knows I've gone. He'll think the kids are gone with me an' he'll leave it alone.

BESSIE: Crap! They gotta go to school haven't they? Won't take him long to know they're still around. So you see it ain't no use you goin' off to Philadelphia on your own.

LAURA: She just don't want to look after them that's all.

BESSIE: Not my responsibility.

LAURA: Their own grannie. An' she talks about how bad colored folks is. Well Lindy took 'em in when I asked her. No questions. Just took 'em in.

BESSIE: You payin' her to look after them?

LAURA: I haven't got any money.

BESSIE: Took them out of the kindness of her heart.

LAURA: Yeah, that's right. Lindy's like that. Do anything for anybody.

BESSIE: She payin' for your Amtrak ticket to Philadelphia?

LAURA: How can I have a conversation with her when she's like this? She twists everything I say!

BESSIE: You said you ain't got no money. I ain't got no money. All I'm askin' is who's gonna pay Amtrak or Greyhound or whatever to get you to Philadelphia?

LAURA: I'm sorry I even mentioned fucking Philadelphia!

BESSIE: Now she has to swear.

LAURA: Are you surprised? You're enough to make a saint swear.

BESSIE: What've I said? I'm just tryin' to work things out the best way for all concerned, that's all. You ain't walkin' to Philadelphia.

LAURA: Do you know what it's like to get a feelin' inside you want to kill somebody?

SHARON: I think it's time to go fetch the presents out the car. Why don't you do that?

LAURA glares at BESSIE's back as she stalks out. SHARON waits till she has gone along the veranda.

SHARON: Okay, let's have it... what is all this really about?

BESSIE: She's up to something. You know what it is?

SHARON: Up to something? How would I know?

BESSIE: You're sisters. You've always been close. She tells you things.

SHARON: No, mother, she doesn't tell me things. She doesn't listen to anything I say and she doesn't tell me things. Laura is her own woman, always has been.

BESSIE: I sure would like to know what's going on. Goin' to Philadelphia. Never heard such nonsense in my life.

SHARON: Maybe she just wants to make a new start, get right away from here. I'd say that's pretty natural.

BESSIE: I'd say it's goddam stupid. I'd say it's about the stupidest thing I heard in a long time. Well I ain't bringing her back. I got no savings now to afford somethin' like that. And I ain't gettin' into debt over it neither. I ain't borrowin' thousands of dollars. The state will have to pay for it. She'll be buried in a pauper's grave.

SHARON: What in Christ's name are you talking about?

BESSIE: Don' blaspheme! You want to take the Lord's name in vain, don't do it in my house.

SHARON: We're getting mighty religious all of a sudden aren't we? What are you working yourself up for? You're talking crazy... pauper's grave... what pauper's grave?

BESSIE: The one your sister's gonna be buried in. Well I won't know anything about it. I won't know a thing. She'll die among strangers so there'll be no shame. I'll just forget her. Laura Peterson? Don't know nobody of that name. Sorry, Sherriff, never heard of her. Who's Laura Peterson?

SHARON: Mom, she's your daughter, and she isn't dead.

BESSIE: Might as well be. I know what'll happen to her in Philadelphia. You talk to her, Sharon. Please! You talk to her. Make her see what she's lettin' herself in for.

SHARON: *(Soothingly.)* I'll talk to her.

BESSIE: Men! Goddam Ray Peterson!

SHARON: *(Getting up.)* Would you like a drink now?

BESSIE: Why not?

SHARON: *(Pauses to lay a hand on her mother's shoulder.)* She'll be all right. Don't you worry. She's had a bad time that's all. I'll talk to her.

She moves on. LAURA reappears and enters the room. She carries three seperately wrapped packages and a carrier bag.

LAURA: You ain't labelled them. How we supposed to know which one's which?

BESSIE: What you givin' presents for anyway? To-day's not the day for presents. Christmas Day, birthdays, mother's day, not Thanksgiving.

SHARON: I just felt like it, all right? If you don't want them I'll take them back.

LAURA: Which is which?

SHARON: *(Takes the carrier bag and puts it down.)* Candy for the kids. The big one's for gran'ma. The next biggest is ma's. The little one's yours.

LAURA: Can we open them now?

SHARON: Why not?

LAURA: We didn't get you anything.

SHARON: Didn't expect anything. Like ma says, to-day ain't the day for presents is it? Anyway, I'm eating Thanksgiving dinner with you. That's enough.

BESSIE: Why don't you take your gran'ma's present out to her? Leave it much longer she'll be dead. Won't be no use to her then will it?

LAURA: I think she's asleep.

BESSIE: Oh, well then, let her sleep. *(Feeling the parcel.)* What is it?

SHARON: It's a shawl. Aren't you going to open yours?

BESSIE nods, starts to open her present. LAURA has already ripped open the wrapping on hers to reveal a jewellery box. She opens the box and takes out a pair of cheap earrings, holds them up.

LAURA: Oh, they're pretty!

SHARON: You like them?

LAURA: *(Holding one against her ear.)* Oh, yeah, they're beautiful! Thank you.

SHARON: I thought something pretty would cheer you up a little. You always did like pretty things. Thought they might go with your rhinestone.

LAURA: Oh, yeah! I gotta see what they look like.

She runs from the room. BESSIE has now opened her present and has taken out a small, inexpensive picture frame. She places it on the table and takes out another. There are three altogether.

SHARON: Well?

BESSIE: What're they for?

SHARON: They're picture frames!

BESSIE: I can see they're picture frames. What're they for?

SHARON: I thought you'd like to put your grandchildren's school pictures in them?

BESSIE: What school pictures? Never got any.

SHARON: Oh.

BESSIE: Where you think we're gonna find dollars for school pictures?

Silence.

SHARON: I'm sorry. Well, maybe next year.

BESSIE: Yeah. Maybe next year.

SHARON: You could put in something else meantime.

BESSIE: Like what?

SHARON: You must have some old photos lying around.

Silence.

I tell you what you could do. You could find some pictures in a magazine. Cut them out.

BESSIE: Yeah. I could do that.

LAURA reappears in the doorway. She is blazing mad.

LAURA: Where is it?

BESSIE: *(Calmly.)* Where is what?

LAURA: My rhinestone. You took my rhinestone.

BESSIE: Never touched it.

LAURA: Liar!

BESSIE: Did you look for it real good?

LAURA: What's the point? It's gone! You know it's gone!

BESSIE: If it's gone...

LAURA: IT HAS GONE!

BESSIE: ...then one of your kids must've took it.

LAURA: My kids don't steal! *(She turns to SHARON.)* She took it! Took my rhinestone! Traded it in for a turkey. It was the only thing I had. *(Turns to BESSIE.)* How could you do that?

BESSIE: We got to live on somethin' haven't we? What do you think it costs to feed you an' three growin' kids? I ain't got nothin'. I already sold most everythin'. Sold all the good land. What's left is all rock, fit for nothin' but sheep grazin', an' there's plenty like that around so who'd want more?

LAURA: I gave you my welfare. Gave you my food stamps. *(Pointing outside.)* You got her foodstamps too. Are we so poor we got to steal from each other?

BESSIE: I never stole a thing in my whole life an' I never stole your rhinestone. I borrowed it.

LAURA: Oh, get real! What you mean you borrowed it?

BESSIE goes over to a shelf on which are some old letters, papers, accounts. She hands a slip of paper to LAURA.

BESSIE: Here.

LAURA: What's this?

BESSIE: What's it look like? It's a pawn ticket. You want your rhinestone, go an' get it.

LAURA: How much did they give you for it?

BESSIE: It's all there. Was worth a bit more'n I thought. Seems like the chain is gold. So instead of payin' out good money for that bus ticket to Philadelphia you can go get your rhinestone.

LAURA: Really? How'm I supposed to do that? I told you, I haven't got any money.

SHARON: Oh yes you have.

LAURA: What?

SHARON: How about the money I gave you to get the kids' school photographs?

LAURA: Medical expenses!

SHARON: What medical expenses?

LAURA: For the ringworm. For the kids.

SHARON: Oh yes?

LAURA: I told you, the dogs got the ringworm. The kids got it from the dogs. I had to take them to the doctor. Pay for medication.

BESSIE: What medication?

LAURA: Ointment.

BESSIE: You're lyin' again. The clinic would've given you

LAURA: that.

LAURA: You want to see the receipts?

SHARON: Forget it. It doesn't matter. Let's just calm down now. If Glen ever finds out about that thirty seven dollars he'll probably shoot me. He won't say anything. He'll just take down his gun, look me straight between the eyes, and shoot me.

LAURA: I'm sorry.

SHARON: You will be if he shoots me. Fortunately he never knew I had the money in the first place.

LAURA: I'll get the photos.

SHARON: And I'll get another drink. *(She proceeds to do so.)* I must've been crazy. What'd I do it for? I can give away thirty seven dollars just like that? That's a whole heap of money.

LAURA: I'm sorry, Sharon.

SHARON: Quit saying you're sorry! Bein' sorry's no good to anyone.

LAURA: As soon as I get a job I'll pay you back. Out of my very first wages. I promise. An' I'll get the photos so you can have some. That's what you wanted isn't it?

SHARON: It's so unfair. So goddam unfair.

LAURA: How am I goin' to get my rhinestone back?

SHARON: If you say one more word about your crappy rhinestone I'll get it back for you, and I'll put it round your scrawny neck, and I'll pull it so tight you'll wish you hadn't got it back!

LAURA: Don't be mad at me, Sharon, please! Don't be mad.

SHARON sighs deeply and takes a drink.

BESSIE: *(Rewrapping the frames.)* Guess I might as well put these away. Got no use for them now. Thanks to my youngest daughter.

LAURA stands for a moment, looking from one to the other, then runs from the room in tears.

SHARON raises her glass in a toast.

SHARON: Happy Thanksgiving.

ACT TWO

The meal preparations are advanced an hour which means the sink is full of dirty bowls, pans, utensils. The table is cleared. There are pots on top of the stove and, presumably, the turkey is still in the oven.

SHARON is standing, glass in hand, staring out of a window.

Gran'ma's present is still in evidence.

LAURA appears at the inner door, pauses to survey SHARON's back and then advances into the room, going straight for her cigarettes.

SHARON turns around.

SHARON: Feeling better?

LAURA nods, goes to the stove, turns it on under the coffee pot, sniffs loudly, looks around.

LAURA: Where's ma?

SHARON: Layin' down. *(Pause.)* You want to talk?

LAURA shrugs, pulls on her cigarette.

Well?

LAURA: Well what?

SHARON: Are we going to talk or just look at each other? *(Silence.)* You want to talk, Laura. Don't you? So why don't you just do it?

LAURA: Talk about what?

SHARON: Oh, God!

LAURA: I am going you know.

SHARON: Sure.

LAURA: Whether she likes it or not. She's not stoppin' me. If she won't take the kids...

SHARON: Why should she? Like she says, they're not her responsibility. An' I don't blame her, at her age. They ain't her kids. She's had the responsibility of bringing up kids. She don't need it all over again. She wouldn't want it all over again. She'd be scared of it.

LAURA: It won't be for long.

SHARON: You don't know that. Could be a long while. Kids need watchin', lookin' after all the time at their age. Fallin' down, gettin' into scrapes, gettin' sick...

LAURA: Oh, what do you know about it?

SHARON: She's too old for that now.

LAURA: Okay then, I'll leave them with Lindy. Lindy'll take care of them.

SHARON: What's the matter with you, Laura? You think they're puppies to be given away? They're your kids for God's sake!

LAURA: I ain't givin' them away. All I'm doin' is askin' somebody to look after them for a while. That's all.

SHARON: Oh, is that all? Well it's time you got clued up. You think Lindy ain't got enough to do lookin' after her own without taking on yours?

LAURA: Would you take them?

SHARON: You know better'n to ask me that.

LAURA: You would if you could though, wouldn't you?

	(Silence.) Ain't you ever gonna have kids of your own, Sharon? *(No answer.)* Ain't ya?
SHARON:	No, Laura, I guess not.
LAURA:	Why not? That's what you got married for, isn't it? You always said how you wanted kids of... your own.
SHARON:	Drop it, Laura. Just shut up about it, okay?
LAURA:	Is it because Glen hates them?
SHARON:	What!
LAURA:	I seen him when kids is around. They get too close, he looks at them, they go away. They don't come back again. They know he hates them. Maybe if he had kids of his own...
SHARON:	He can't.
LAURA:	What?
SHARON:	He can't have them.
LAURA:	HE can't have them?
SHARON:	That's what I just said. Oh, I know what you been thinking, what everybody's been thinking, but it's not my fault.
LAURA:	You mean Glen can't do it?
SHARON:	No, Laura, that's not what I mean.
LAURA:	Well then... has he been checked out?
SHARON:	Won't go. I tried. Gave up. You can't talk to a man who gets up, puts on his hat, and walks out the room. But I got myself checked out. Got the results a couple a days back. I can have kids. Nothing

	wrong. Everything in the right place, everything in perfect working order, everything waiting. For what? I won't ever have one.
LAURA:	That's too bad, Sharon.
SHARON:	Anyway, I thought we're supposed to be talking about you. I've told you my secret, now tell me yours.
LAURA:	*(A little laugh.)* Secret? I ain't got no secret.
SHARON:	You had secrets all your life. You got one now. You gonna tell?
LAURA:	I got plans. I made no secret of that. I'm going to Philadelphia.
SHARON:	Who with?

Pause.

LAURA:	What?
SHARON:	You heard me. Who you going with?
LAURA:	What makes you think I'm goin' with anyone?
SHARON:	Because it's not your idea.
LAURA:	Who says so?
SHARON:	I say so. Somebody's put the idea into your head and that somebody is either taking you or going with, so who is it?
LAURA:	Why can't it be my idea? Don't see why it's got to be somebody else gives me the idea.
SHARON:	It's too big an idea for you. Somebody's putting you up to it.

LAURA: And somebody's puttin' you up to askin' all these questions. It's her. She said to you to ask me, when I went out to the car, to get the presents. I know exactly what she said, "She's up to something. Find out." That's what she said, didn't she?

SHARON: Sure. But even if she hadn't I'd still like to know. I'm... interested. I'd like to know who the new man in your life is, how long you been seeing him, what he's like. Is it someone I know? Come on, Laura.

LAURA: Shit! You're a cow, Sharon!

LAURA turns to the stove, lifts the lid off the coffee pot, peeks inside, moves across to join SHARON at the table, stubs out her cigarette. Gets up, goes to the inner door, closes it, returns to the table, sits, gets up, goes back to the stove, picks up a cup, pours herself a coffee, returns to the table and sits where she can watch the door. SHARON follows it all without moving.

SHARON: Well?

LAURA: Mom wants me to get married again.

SHARON: You ain't even divorced yet.

LAURA: After the divorce.

SHARON: Well of course. We wouldn't want to add bigamy to your problems would we? Who's she got in mind?

LAURA: *(Laughing.)* How did you know?

SHARON: I know my ma just as well as I know you, little sister. So who is he, Laura?

LAURA: *(Takes a sip of coffee and pulls a face.)* Ugh! That is gross.

She gets up, takes the cup over to the sink and gets rid of the coffee. Then she stands for a moment, looking out of the window.

Will you look at that sky! We're gonna have a sunset.

SHARON: To the best of my knowledge the sun does that every day.

LAURA: The trees are late turnin' this year. It's the warm weather. Oh, look! There's a cardinal. And there's his mate!

SHARON: Why don't you go out and have a conversation with them? You obviously don't want to talk to me.

LAURA: I do! I do! *(She goes over to the fridge, takes out a bottle of pop, opens it.)* I do want to talk to you, Sharon. You're the only person I can talk to, 'cept for Lindy. *(She goes back to the table, looks SHARON straight in the eyes.)*

SHARON: Then who is it?

A beat.

LAURA: It's Henry.

A beat.

SHARON: Henry Johnson?

LAURA nods.

Oh, my God, Laura!

LAURA: You don't have to sound so shocked. It happens you know. *(She takes a drink from the bottle.)* I love him... I think... *(Starting to howl)* ...I love Ray! I still love Ray!

SHARON: *(Taking her hand.)* Okay, baby, okay...shhhhhh...

LAURA: Hic! Oh, shit! I drunk too fast. Now I got hiccups.

SHARON: Hold your breath. Take a deep breath and hold it long as you can.

LAURA does so.

How long?

LAURA: How long?

SHARON: How long have you been dating... seeing... Henry Johnson?

LAURA: Oh, I thought you were talking about my breath. How you expect me to hold my breath, hic! If you keep askin' me, hic! questions?

SHARON: *(Moving away, taking her glass with her.)* I need another drink.

LAURA: Hey, Sharon, you ain't drivin' home tonight. How many drinks you had an' we ain't even ate yet? Hic! Maybe I need a drink. Maybe it'll get rid of the hiccups. Will you, hic! fix me one please?

SHARON: Sure.

LAURA: Thanks.

SHARON fixes the drink. LAURA sits at the table, hiccupping. SHARON hands her the drink.

LAURA: Thanks.

SHARON: You're welcome.

SHARON takes a mouthful of her drink. LAURA takes a delicate sip.

How long have you been seeing Henry?

LAURA:	A while.
SHARON:	How long is a while?
LAURA:	I don't keep a diary.
SHARON:	Smart. Where?
LAURA:	At the house.
SHARON:	Lindy's house?
LAURA:	Well that's where he lives isn't it?
SHARON:	Nowhere else?
LAURA:	Where else is there?
SHARON:	Well thank God for that. At least you got the excuse you've been going to see Lindy.
LAURA:	I don't need excuses for going anywhere, not anymore.
SHARON:	Laura! Henry Johnson is black!
LAURA:	Holy shit, Sharon! Hic! You think, Hic!, think I don't know that? Am I blind or something? Henry is Lindy's brother. Lindy is black, Henry is black. Lindy's husband was black, Lindy's mother is black. Lindy's kids is black. My God, they're all black, and I love all of them. 'Cept for Lindy's husband that is who I ain't never met.
SHARON:	*(Shaking her head.)* You can't do this, Laura. Jesus, God! You can't do this!
LAURA:	Why not?
SHARON:	You know damn well why not.
LAURA:	No I don't.

SHARON: Who are you kidding? I can just hear what Glen would say for a start. No I can't. He wouldn't say anything. But I know what he would be thinking. And what about Ray? And the rest of the Petersons, that whole damn family? Plus all their friends and relations. Leave Ray to go with a black man? What about all Ray's bar buddies? Are you out of your mind? Think about it, Laura, for Henry's sake, if not your own.

LAURA: It's his fault.

SHARON: Whose?

LAURA: Ray's.

SHARON: Who gives a rat's ass whose fault it is? When the shit starts hittin' the fan you better start runnin'. Who else knows about this? Anybody?

LAURA shakes her head.

Lindy's kids know!

LAURA: What do they know?

SHARON: Kids know. And kids talk to other kids and other kids talk to their folks.

LAURA: Hic!

SHARON: And what about ma? You think for one minute your mother's gonna accept a black man for her son-in-law you better think again.

LAURA: That is why we want to go to Philadelphia. Nobody knows us there.

SHARON: Look, Laura...

LAURA: Hic!

SHARON: Will you stop doing that?

LAURA: I can't help it. I'm not doin' it on purpose.

SHARON: Put your head between your knees.

LAURA does so.

Now listen to me and listen up real good... right this minute you don't know what you rightly want. You're all mixed up. You can't go back to Ray, that's for sure, not after all those things he done to you.

LAURA: I could end up dead if I went back to him.

SHARON: I know you still feel... well, you know... you say you still feel for him, Ray, and that's got you all confused. Laura, I can't talk to the top of your head! Aren't you feeling any better?

LAURA: *(Sits up and waits.)* Yes.

SHARON: Good.

LAURA: Hic! No.

SHARON goes to the fridge for an ice cube, comes back with it.

SHARON: Why, Laura? What's the attraction? What do you see in him?

LAURA: That's a dumb question. God, that is so stupid! What do you see in Glen? I ain't never figured that one out. An' now you told me what you tole me 'bout him I still can't figure it out, but that's your business. I love him. Oh, maybe not the same way as I love Ray I guess but I know what mama means. I know what she was talkin' about. Ow! What the fuck are you doin'?

SHARON has slipped the ice-cube down the back of LAURA's dress. LAURA leaps to her feet, twisting and turning.

SHARON: It's only an ice cube.

LAURA: Get it out! Get it out! It's freezing!

SHARON: That's the idea.

LAURA: Will you get it out of there? Get it out!

SHARON: Okay.

She retrieves the ice, takes it back to the sink.

LAURA: You're nuts.

SHARON: Hiccups gone?

LAURA: *(Stands for a moment.)* Yeh.

SHARON: Good. Now, what were you saying about mama?

LAURA: She... when she was talkin' about how I should get married again... Shit, Sharon! I'm all wet.

SHARON: It'll dry.

LAURA: Well. She said I should find someone who's different.

SHARON: I don't think she was referring to color.

LAURA: That's not funny, Sharon.

SHARON: Sorry.

LAURA stands glaring at her.

I'm sorry.

LAURA makes a big deal of trying to wriggle the wet dress off her back.

LAURA: She said to find a man so ain't I doin' what mama wanted?

SHARON: Except with the wrong man.

LAURA: No, Sharon. He treats me right. He's kind an' gentle, an' smilin' all the time. An' he loves kids. An' they love him. They're all over him, all the time. Over his knees, on his shoulders, round his neck. An' not one at a time. One gets there they all gotta get there, crawlin' all over him. Like puppies. An' he doesn't mind, doesn't kick 'em off. You know what a big man he is, an' they're pullin' at him, tuggin', an' it's uncle Henry here an' uncle Henry this, an' he's smilin' all the time, an' looks over at me an' I know what he's thinkin'. He's not thinkin' sex, you know, sex. He's thinkin' love, an' that makes me smile. Then he looks away, back to the tv maybe, or maybe across to Lindy an' he makes her smile too because she knows what a lovin' kind of man he is. And I feel... Oh, shit, Sharon! What's it got to do with other people? What's it got to do with anybody 'cept ourselves? But I know what it would be like, stayin' here. Don't need you to tell me that. That's why we're plannin' on Philadelphia. And I can't tell mama, she wouldn't understand. It could kill her. Oh, Sharon...

LAURA stands there, a distraught, helpless figure until SHARON puts her arm around her, holds her, strokes her hair.

SHARON: It's okay... okay... come on now.

The door opens and BESSIE enters.

BESSIE: What the hell's goin' on in here? Why's this door shut? An' whatsa matter with her?

SHARON: She's upset.

BESSIE: What about?

SHARON: A whole lot of things. Marriage breaking up, don't know what to do, which way to turn. Wouldn't you be upset?

BESSIE crosses over to the stove, opens the oven, looks in, closes it. LAURA pulls away from SHARON, wipes the tears away with the back of her hand, wipes her nose with her finger.

Want a hankie?

LAURA shakes her head, gives her cheek another wipe, sniffs.

BESSIE: All right now? Feelin' better?

LAURA nods, picks up gran'ma's present.

LAURA: We should give gran'ma her present.

BESSIE: *(Taking the parcel from her.)* She's all right. Leave her be. Why don't you go wash your face? Go on, it'll make you feel better.

LAURA goes.

Plenty of cold water, splash it on real good, get all the red outa your eyes.

SHARON picks up the parcel and turns to go.

Where you goin'?

SHARON: Give gran'ma her present.

BESSIE: Leave it. By the time you give it her an' explain it'll take half an hour an' she'll still think it's Christmas. She can get it when she comes in. We'll put it over her when she's in bed.

SHARON: We ought to bring her in. It's getting a mite chilly out there.

BESSIE: In a minute. What did Laura tell you?

SHARON: Nothing.

BESSIE: SHA-ron...

SHARON: Nothing.

BESSIE: Then what's she so upset about? You must've been talkin' about somethin' to make her so upset.

SHARON: I didn't get her upset. She is upset. And I told you why. It's going to be a long time before she gets over Ray, before she forgets him.

BESSIE: The sooner she forgets him the better. Pickin' at sores don't heal 'em.

SHARON: It's not as easy as that is it? When did you stop pickin' at yours?

BESSIE: What's that supposed to mean?

SHARON: You know what I'm talking about.

BESSIE: No, I don't know what you're talkin' about. You might know what you're talking about. I don't.

SHARON: What I'm talking about is her... out there.

BESSIE: You leave her out of it. You don't understand.

SHARON: And you don't understand Laura so why don't you just leave her out of it? Let her sort her own life in her own way. It's her life.

BESSIE: Done a pretty good job of sortin' it out so far hasn't she?

SHARON: Reckon you haven't been much help.

BESSIE: I don't believe this. I don't believe what I'm hearin' here. What's she been tellin' you? Why you sayin' these things to me? Makin' out like it's all my fault.

SHARON: I didn't say it was all your fault.

BESSIE: I just heard you say it!

SHARON: MO-ther...

BESSIE: And don't MO-ther me. I suppose your life's one big bed of roses, huh? And I suppose I'm to blame for that as well. I don't know why God didn't make kids just like other animals. You give them the tit till they're weaned then you kick 'em out. Every time they come whinin' back you give 'em a kick in the heinie 'till they don't come back no more. By the time they've growed you wouldn't know them if you saw them. I suppose it was me forced you into marryin' Glen Palmer.

SHARON: Nobody forced me into marryin' anyone. And I ain't complainin'. You ever hear me complain? Give me one time.

BESSIE: No, I gotta admit, I never did hear you complain. But then you ain't the complainin' type. Never did, not even when you was a little girl. *(Pointedly.)* You're the kind quietly drowns her sorrows.

SHARON: I'm drinking because this is Thanksgiving Day and this family is driving me to it.

BESSIE: Couldn't help noticin'. Well you'd best not drive with all that inside you.

SHARON: Thanks. I've already had that warning today.

BESSIE: I'll make up a spare bed. Glen won't even notice you ain't there. Guess he'll be out all night anyway. He better get one deer before the end of the season or he won't be worth livin' with 'till next fall, seein' as to how he didn't even get a bear neither. I'd ask him to shoot that damn cat but, knowin' his luck, it'd just sit there laughin' in his face.

SHARON: You're having a lovely time aren't you? Is this all because you think Laura told me something and I won't tell you.

BESSIE: I don't give a diddlysquat what she might have told you. You accuse me of not understandin'. How'm I to understand somethin' I don't know nothin' about? If she don't want me to know about it I can't help her, can I?

BESSIE goes over to the sink and starts cleaning up the dishes.

SHARON: I see. Talkin's over is it? Okay, I'll just sit here an' drown my sorrows. You stay over there an' pick your sores. I'll sit here an' bathe mine in alcohol. *(She watches her mother for a moment.)* Ain't no one blaming you, ma. Must've been hard for you, trying to run this place, raise two kids on your own, look after your mother. That's a deal for one body to cope with. Wears a person down. And what have you got to show for it? What's left but an empty barn, a falling down house, junk all over the yard?

BESSIE: Weren't my fault. Prices goin' up all the time. You tell me what a dollar buys nowadays. Then three bad years, one after the other. You get bad years like that what can you do? Bank wouldn't lend. Lost all my Christmas trees in the fire. Used to count on those trees, tide us over the winter. Then the flu wipin' out my turkeys. Now I gotta buy a turkey for Thanksgivin'. Never had to buy a turkey in my life before. Raised 'em. Hundred of 'em. Thousands I reckon. Now I go into a supermarket like other people an' get one, frozen stiff, wrapped in plastic. Meat don't taste the same no more, not like it used to. Can't tell the difference between the meat an' the plastic now.

SHARON:	There's a whole lot more people to feed.
BESSIE:	That's what I was sayin' to Laura. Too many people. An' too many gettin' older all the time, need lookin' after. Soon it will be me. Who's gonna look after me?
SHARON:	If you was to look after Laura's kids now, for a while...
BESSIE:	Can't do it.
SHARON:	They're still your grandchildren, your flesh and blood.
BESSIE:	Bad blood. It ain't the same. That family? I don't have to tell you 'bout them. Trash. Nothin' but trash. In an' out of trouble, in an' out of jail. God! If I'd ha' knowed at the time it was Ray Peterson Laura was seein' down there in the woods I'd ha' peppered his butt with buckshot, while he was on the job, just as he was a comin'. He'd ha' remembered that one for the rest of his days. He'd never have had another one like that, that's for sure. Sassy little skunk... always preenin' hisself, slickin' back his hair, playin' with hisself. Never seen that kid but he didn't have his hand on it, pullin' at his crotch. Makin' sure it was still there I shouldn't wonder, in workin' order. You wanna look after his kids, you look after 'em.

Silence. SHARON fiddles with her glass.

	She still goin' to Philadelphia?
SHARON:	Yeh.
BESSIE:	You believe her? That story 'bout Lindy's friend? Stayin' there? You don't, do you. No more do I.

The room has gotten darker. There is a distinct touch of red in the sky as the sun goes down. LAURA breezes into the room.

LAURA: Talkin about me again? When we eatin'?

BESSIE: When it's good and ready.

LAURA: *(Looking for something to snack on.)* I'm starvin'. What's this? Honey Grahams. That'll do. Got any marshmallows?

BESSIE: No. Can't wait, can you? That was always your trouble. If you'd kept your legs crossed a while longer we wouldn't be sittin' here talking about you, tryin' to figure somethin' out.

LAURA: Like what?

BESSIE: Like what to do with your kids if you're still hankerin' on goin' to Philadelphia.

LAURA: Oh...

She looks at SHARON. SHARON drinks. LAURA takes a bag of tortilla chips from a cupboard and munches on them together with the Honey Grahams. The munching is very loud.

BESSIE: What am I doin' all this cookin' for?

LAURA: When dinner's good an' ready I'll eat it. Smells good. It's the smell's makin' me hungry.

BESSIE: Well why don't you go work up your appetite some more, take a couple of those clean sheets an' make up a bed for your sister. By the look of her she's gonna need it.

SHARON: Ha ha.

BESSIE: Go on. An' take that racket with you. I can't stand people chewin' with their mouth open.

SHARON: And I can't stand crumbs in the bed so don't go

	eatin' chips and crackers while you're doin' it.
LAURA:	*(Brightly as she goes.)* Okay.
BESSIE:	What's she so chirpy 'bout all of a sudden? Got somethin' off her chest?
SHARON:	Ma... if... just supposing now... if Laura... if she was to do something, something that would be good for her... well, you mayn't like it... mayn't understand it...
BESSIE:	She DID tell you somethin'!
SHARON:	Listen... what I'm saying, asking, is...would you be willing to...
BESSIE:	You're runnin' 'round Robin Hood's barn, Sharon. Spit it out.
SHARON:	...try ...try to go along with it, try and see her side, no matter how you might feel about it?
BESSIE:	I don't know what you're sayin'.
SHARON:	I'm trying to make things good between you and Laura... before she goes.
BESSIE:	You mean she ain't comin' back?
SHARON:	Maybe not. And, whatever she's done, might do, she's still your daughter, she's still my sister. Family should stick together, make things easier for each other.
BESSIE:	You're drunk, Sharon.
SHARON:	Not yet.
BESSIE:	You're tellin' me I gotta like somethin' before I even know what it is? Is that it? What kind of a thing is that to ask anyone?

SHARON: Maybe I am drunk.

BESSIE: Are you tryin' to scare me?

SHARON: No, mother.

BESSIE: Then say right out what you gotta say.

SHARON: Forget it. Forget I said anything.

BESSIE: Sharon!

LAURA appears at the door. They both turn to look at her.

LAURA: He's here.

SHARON: What?

LAURA: Ray. He's sittin' on his bike, up the road. I told you he would come didn't I?

BESSIE: What's he doin'?

LAURA: Just sittin' there, on his bike. I went to make the bed for Sharon, I went to close the curtain an' I looked out the window, and there he was. I'm scared.

BESSIE: Nothin' to be scared of if he's just sittin' there.

LAURA: Sharon?

SHARON: Mom's right, Laura. He'll stay there a while then he'll likely move off. He'll see my car anyway, maybe think Glen's here. It's okay, Laura, don't worry.

LAURA: What if he comes down?

SHARON: What if he does? What can he do?

LAURA:	I don't know. He'll have been drinking. You don't know what he's like when he's been drinking.
BESSIE:	He'd best not try anything, not in my house.

She goes for the gun.

LAURA:	You don't know what he'll do. He gets crazy.
SHARON:	Leave that alone, mama. Put it down. There's no need for that.

BESSIE heads for the veranda.

LAURA:	Mama! No! Stop her, Sharon!

SHARON heads her off.

SHARON:	Jesus! You want a murder in this house? Now let's just carry on like nothing's happening. After a while he'll go away, you'll see. Is he on his own?

LAURA nods.

He'll go away.

LAURA goes to the window and looks out.

BESSIE:	What's he doin'?
LAURA:	Just sittin' there. No he's not. He's turnin' his bike.
SHARON:	Told you. He's leaving.
LAURA:	Turned right round. He's comin' down. Oh, God! He's comin'!
SHARON:	*(Slams down her glass.)* Shit! *(Heads for the door.)*
LAURA:	Where you goin'?
SHARON:	To sort out that shithead you call a husband.

LAURA: Don't go out there!

SHARON: Someone's got to sort him out. He's got no right hanging around, scarin' you to death. You stay here. *(To BESSIE.)* See she stays right here.

BESSIE: She ain't goin' no place.

There is the sound of a motor bike. it gets louder. The dogs are barking. The bike cuts out.

SHARON has gone out, disappears along the veranda.

LAURA goes to the sink to look out of the window. She can't see down into the yard so she gets a chair and stands on it.

BESSIE: What's happenin'?

LAURA: Can't see.

BESSIE: *(Moving to the door.)* I'm going out there.

LAURA: No, mama, no! He won't start anything with Sharon. He starts with her, he starts with Glen an' he ain't gonna do that. *(She moves from the chair to kneel on the work surface, right up against the window. She has to push a few things aside to get there.)* He's just sittin' on his bike. Sharon's goin' up to him... they're talkin'... See? It's okay... he's lookin' up at the house... now back to Sharon.

Silence.

BESSIE: What're they doin' now?

LAURA: Still talkin'.

Silence.

BESSIE: Laura... Pssst, Laura!

LAURA:	What?
BESSIE:	You told Sharon something, while I was resting. What was it?
LAURA:	She tell you that?
BESSIE:	No, I guessed at it. Are you in trouble, Laura? Is that why you want to go to Philadelphia?
LAURA:	No. Don't look like they're talkin no more. He's just lookin' straight ahead. Sharon's got her arms folded. You know what that means don'tcha? Ain't no one gonna mess with her.
BESSIE:	Who's messin' with you?
LAURA:	Nobody. Shit! *(Panic)* He's gettin' off his bike. He ain't goin'!

BESSIE heads for the door.

    What you doin'?

BESSIE:	Goin' out there.
LAURA:	No! Stay here Godammit! You go out there we're in real trouble. Sharon can handle it. *(She starts to sound like a sports commentator.)* He's walked round the bike, goin' up to her... dogs' sniffin' his leg... Sharon ain't movin'... yes she is, she's turned away, walkin' away... Holy shit! She's picked up a spade... she's turned back... she's goin' for him... Kee-rist! She's hit him on the head!... dug him in the stomach...

The dogs, excited by the action, start to bark.

    He's goin' back... he's fallen over... fallen over his bike... now the bike's fallen over... dog's got his trousers... he's gettin' up... *(There is the sound of a dog yelping)*...kicked the dog... dog's slunk off.

BESSIE: Is Sharon all right?

LAURA: Sure. He's pickin' up his bike. *(She shrieks with laughter.)* He's fallen over again, bike's heavy. Sharon's just standin' there, watchin'. He's up again... bike's up... he's gettin' on it.

The bike revs into life.

He's goin'.

And roars away.

Told you no one was gonna mess with her. Didn't I tell you? Look at him go! Wowee! *(She scrambles off her perch.)* I'm glad Sharon's drunk. She could ha' killed him if she'd been sober. You should have seen her hit him with that spade.

SHARON appears on the veranda, walks along it, gets to the screen door, opens it, stops, looks to the side. A long moment. BESSIE and LAURA wait until LAURA can't stand it a moment longer.

LAURA: Sharon? What'd he say?

SHARON: Mother, I think you'd better come out here. I think she's dead. Gran'ma's dead.

ACT THREE

Night. The room is empty. Lights on. Everything is as it was except the turkey has been removed from the oven and Gran'ma's present has gone.

After a moment LAURA enters from the house, looks around the room.

LAURA: Sharon? *(She moves further into the room.)* Sharon!

SHARON: *(From the veranda.)* Out here.

LAURA crosses to the outside door, opens the screen, looks out.

LAURA: What you doin' out here?

SHARON: Thinkin'.

LAURA: Why you sittin' in gran'ma's chair?

SHARON: Why not?

LAURA: There's other chairs.

SHARON: So?

LAURA: *(Pause.)* She died in that chair, Sharon.

SHARON: World's full of chairs people have died in.

LAURA: Why don't you come on in? It's cold out here.

SHARON: *(Gets up, stands by the rail.)* Moon's so bright tonight. All those stars. Funny, isn't it? To think there's been men up there. It's so quiet out here. Hasn't been a car on the road for a while.

LAURA: Come on in, Sharon. It's cold.

LAURA holds the screen door open with her body. SHARON

enters the kitchen. LAURA follows her, closing the door.

SHARON: How's ma?

LAURA: *(Looking towards the inner door.)* Okay, I guess.

SHARON picks up her glass, goes over to where the Bourbon bottle still stands, pours herself another drink, gets ice from the fridge.

I wonder how long she was dead before we noticed.

SHARON: Want one?

LAURA: *(Shakes her head.)* No. What do you think she died of?

SHARON: Body's eighty years old and more what do you think she died of?

LAURA: She looks so peaceful lyin' there. She died real peaceful, that's somethin'.

SHARON closes the fridge door, goes to the sink to add water.

Hope when I die I go that easy. Must've just slipped away, not a sound, like goin' into a nice quiet sleep.

SHARON: Maybe we shouldn't have moved her.

LAURA: Why not?

SHARON: I don't know. Authorities are going to want to poke around, find out what she died of.

LAURA: We couldn't leave her out there. *(Pause.)* Your present looks nice round her shoulders. It's a pretty shawl. Where'd you get it?

SHARON: Thrift shop.

LAURA: I thought it must be old...the fringe...the roses.

	Looks Spanish. You think it might be Spanish? Mexican maybe.
SHARON:	Probably made in Japan.
LAURA:	It's a pretty shawl though. Guess she'll be buried in it, huh? That'd be nice.
SHARON:	*(Holding up the near depleted bourbon bottle.)* We're the kind of people other people complain about, using their welfare for liquor and cigarettes. *(She puts down the bottle.)* Still going to Philadelphia?

LAURA nods.

	What about mama?
LAURA:	What about her?
SHARON:	She's on her own now.
LAURA:	You think gran'ma's dyin's gonna make a difference to mama?
SHARON:	Someone dyin' always makes a difference no matter what. Dyin' is the end, the last good-bye. If not, too bad. Too late anymore to make up, say you're sorry about things, say how much you really loved a person.
LAURA:	Mama wouldn't do that anyway. She hated her. Treated her real bad, Sharon, you know that. She was cruel, the things she said, the things she did. Why? Why did she hate her so much? I hope nobody ever hates me as much as that. Maybe it's true what Ray said.
SHARON:	What was that?
LAURA:	*(Shrugs.)* Dirty things. Things you don't talk about.

SHARON: Like what?

LAURA: Says he heard his folks talkin'. Says everybody knows about it.

SHARON: Knows about what?

LAURA: Oh, Sharon, not now. She's only just gone. Shouldn't speak evil of the dead anyway.

SHARON: God! You're the most aggravating creature sometimes, Laura.

LAURA: Don't you feel anything for her? Don't you feel sad? Sorry?

SHARON: No. *(She goes to the table, taking the bottle with her, sits down, adds the last of the liquor to her glass.)* In a way it's a good thing. She had to go sometime, why not now? Reckon she was more'n likely pleased it had come at last. Should have been in a home really, not bein' able to do anything for herself. I hope I never get like that. Would have been easier if we'd had money.

LAURA: Money would make a whole lot of things easier.

SHARON: There's only one thing left to sell and that's this house, and what's in it. And there's nobody, but nobody's going to buy this shack. Well look at it, it's falling down. And nobody, but nobody's going to want this junk.

LAURA: Sharon!

SHARON: This junk! Look at it, Laura. You see anything in here even worth giving away? And the rest of the house is no better.

LAURA: What's gonna happen then?

SHARON: I don't know. And, right this minute, I don't care.

LAURA:	You're drunk.
SHARON:	Everybody keeps telling me I'm drunk. I am not drunk. I'm celebrating.

LAURA snorts.

	And what am I celebrating? I'm celebrating Thanksgiving day. *(She laughs.)*
LAURA:	Sharon! There's death in this house an' all you can do is sit there knocking back that stuff.
SHARON:	Oh what a good little girl we are all of a sudden. So righteous. We'll be saying our prayers next, reading the good book. Death scared you, has it?
LAURA:	No. First time I ever seen a dead body. Don't scare me though, not lookin' like that, like she's asleep. Hard to believe she's dead though. I looked at her an' I thought, she's smilin' I thought. An' I swear her eyelids moved, Sharon. So I looked at her hand an' I could ha' sworn her hand moved. I wanted to tell her, "Come on now, gran'ma, wake up. We're gonna eat soon. It's Thanksgiving dinner." Hard to believe a body can lay there so still, not movin' at all. Seed no reason why she couldn't come with me. She'd open her eyes, I'd sit her up, put her in her wheelchair, bring her out here. I looked at her mouth an' she was smilin'. Why am I cryin'? Why am I cryin'? She didn't mean nothin' to me, was just someone who was around, like an' old tree, like an old animal. You said, "Hi, gran'ma, how ya doin' gran'ma? Bye, gran'ma" but you didn't expect her to say anythin' back, didn't expect her to know you was even there. She was just an old nuisance, havin' to feed her, change her, put her to bed, get her up, like a big overgrown baby. I'm glad too, glad she's gone, so why am I cryin'?
SHARON:	Shock. *(She slides her glass across the table.)* Have

	some of this.
LAURA:	No.
SHARON:	It'll help.
LAURA:	No. I got other things to think about.
SHARON:	Tell me what Ray said about her.
LAURA:	Not just about her, but about gran'pa, an' mama.

BESSIE appears at the door. They don't see her.

	Sharon, if you really want to know, maybe I should tell you sometime when you ain't so full of whiskey.
SHARON:	No, tell me now, dammit! I want to know now!
LAURA:	Well... okay then... when mama an' her sister Dorcus was little, this is how Ray tells it, I mean, what he heard from his folks, so I don't know.
SHARON:	For Chrissakes, Laura! Will you get on with it?
LAURA:	Well I don't exactly know how old mama was at the time...
BESSIE:	Nine.
LAURA:	Mama!
BESSIE:	I was nine years old. I remember it like it was today because it happened on my ninth birthday.
LAURA:	*(Who has gotten up.)* Mama, you all right?
BESSIE:	I had a birthday party, right here, in this kitchen.
SHARON:	Come and sit down, ma.

LAURA: Here... *(Pushing her chair forward.)*

But BESSIE crosses to the stove for a cup of coffee.

BESSIE: Right here, in this very room. It weren't much of a party of course, not to speak of. We were better off in them days but still it weren't much. But, oh, the excitement! Me an' Dorcus in our best party clothes... *(She turns around to survey the room.)*... The room was different then, everythin' fresher, newer. Your grandad had just painted it. She'd gone on at him somethin' fierce. "When you gonna paint this kitchen for me, Earl? I been askin' an' askin' an' you keep on sayin' as to how you're gonna get round to it an' you never do. Never do anythin' I ask, try to make things better for me." Well it ain't that simple to take time off from everythin' needs doin' round a farm to mess about paintin' kitchens an' he told her so. But he must've growed tired of her naggin' an' one day he brung back a couple of them paint charts from Charlottesville an' we all sat round the table choosin' the colors. *(She sits.)* An' finally, we decided on buttercup an' a pale blue. Daddy went on back into Charlottesville an' picked up the paint. We waited out there for him to get back. He took off the lids of those cans with a screwdriver an' I remember how disappointed we was. The paint was like an oily brown. An' daddy laughed and said how you gotta stir it real good. Paint them days weren't like it is today. You stirred an' stirred an' you had to be real careful how you put it on too. A tad too much an' you'd have slicks all runnin' down. An', if you didn't paint all one ways, you could see the brush marks. An' it took so long to dry. An' the whole house smelled so of paint, mama said she was movin' out cause it was givin' her a headache. And how could she use a kitchen stunk so? But he got it done in time for the party an' we all stood over there by the door lookin' at it. It was real pretty, buttercup an' pale blue, only she didn't seem none too grateful. I couldn't understand why at the time. "It'll do," was all she said. Paint smell had near gone by my birthday. The table was laid out all nice and pretty, paper plates an' napkins, and a cake with icin' an' little candles on it. They was stuck in those pins with pink and blue roses to hold them, eight round the outside, one in the middle. Your grandad gave me a present, a bracelet, silver bracelet, an' she gave me a pocket book, an' Dorcus had saved up all her pennies an' bought me a whole bunch of my favorite candy. And we had the old wind-up gramophone so there was music. *(Singing.)* "I'm sittin' on top of the world, just rollin' along, just singin' a song." That was on the old Parlaphone label I recall. Or maybe it was Brunswick. Doesn't matter anyways, it was one of my favorites. Seemed to be the right thing for a birthday party. Played it over and over till she said to stop. Said it was givin' her a headache listen' to the same song over an' over an' how she would get to hate it. So we put on "Dancin' Cheek to Cheek." You ever heard that one? *(Singing.)* "Heaven, I'm in heaven..." An' I reckon I was too, all the excitement an' waiting for people to arrive. She said I was gonna make myself sick an' miss my own party if'n I didn't settle down. *(She gets up and goes towards the outer door.)* Party was set for two o'clock. That's when they'd all arrive, friends, mothers, all in their party best, the girls in pretty dresses, ribbons in their hair, some of the boys with bow ties maybe, wearin' shoes, smellin' of brilliantine. So it comes two o'clock and' we waited.

Silence. She looks from one to the other. They are both watching her.

An' guess what?... Nobody came. Nobody. Daddy didn't know what to say to me, couldn't explain it, couldn't tell me the reason why. We sat here, waitin', every now an' again lookin' up there at that ole clock. You remember the ole clock we used to have up there? Watched it tickin' away, pendulum swingin' behind the glass door. Finally daddy got up an' walked out there onto the veranda an' I could see he was cryin'. Then down into the yard, an' then into the barn. His little girl had been hurt an' he didn't know what to say to her, didn't know how to make it better. It was all her fault an' all he could do was go out there into the barn by hisself an' cry.

She is very close to breaking herself. SHARON stretches out a hand but BESSIE pulls away.

No, I'm all right. I ran up to my room and cried too, not just for me, but for him. I'd knowed a long time somethin' was wrong but I was too young to know what. Dorcus came up to me. She brung me some of the food on a paper plate but I couldn't eat it. Then, later, I heard yellin' down here an' I came down. It was them, fightin', sayin' terrible things to each other, tearin' at each other. He was callin' her all kinds a names, tellin' her as to how it was all her doin', everyone knew what she was up to, an' how did they expect respectable folk to let their kids come to this house, even if it was just for another kid's birthday party? In them days you couldn't play round like folk do now. You played around everyone got to talkin', everyone got to know about it. You was called a loose woman. Other women got scared for their husbands. She didn't care. Didn't give two hoots what nobody said. Well, next morning she was gone. At first Dorcus an' me didn't even ask where she was. Too scared I reckon. Then, when Dorcus did ask him, all he said was she'd gone an' most likely weren't comin' back. She took his car! Took daddy's 1939 Chevrolet an' disappeared. Short time after, her fancy man up an' left his wife an' took off too.

LAURA: Who was it?

BESSIE: You don't need to know. The wife died a while back an' the rest of the family all moved away so it don't matter.

SHARON: But she came back. When did she come back? Seems to me like she's always been around.

BESSIE: Little time after your gran'father died... *(To SHARON)* ...you was about three years old then an' your father was runnin' the farm real well. Well, one day, there she was, standin' by the door. Don't know how long she'd been standin' there. I was cooking at the time I remember. We'd been out all mornin' lookin' for wild mushrooms and we'd got a whole mess; morrels, chicken mushrooms. I was makin' a sauce an' I got a splash on my arm. It burned. I wiped it off an' turned round to get the butter off the table to put on it an' there she was, just standin' there. Oh, what a scare she gave me. We stood a long whiles lookin' at each other and then she said, "And which one are you?" and I said, "I'm Bessie", and she said, after a while lookin' some more, "Don't you know me? I'm your mother." An' that's how she come back. She looked so old, so scrawny, an' her clothes so shabby. All she had was one ole suitcase which she'd put down on the floor next to her. All those years.

LAURA: So you let her stay.

BESSIE: Couldn't do nothin' else.

LAURA: Why not?

BESSIE: Was her place.

SHARON: What!

BESSIE: Sure. That's why she come back. To claim her inheritance.

SHARON: Her place? How come?

BESSIE: Well, your grandad never did make out a will, said he didn't see no sense in it. An' they never did get

	divorced. So the place was hers. She got to hear how he was dead and she come back for it. Said as to how your father was doin' such a fine job we might as well stay on so long as she had a roof over her head for the rest of her days. She'd have had to hire somebody otherwise, or sell up. So you see, there was nothing I could do about it.
SHARON:	And I thought, all these years, you were keeping her.
BESSIE:	Nope. Until today this was her place. Now I reckon, at last, it's legally and rightfully mine. Would have gone to Dorcus if she'd still been with us. Now there ain't no other next of kin in my generation.
LAURA:	An' that's why you hated her so much?
BESSIE:	You know that ain't the reason for it. You know what your Ray's been tellin' you is the real reason. Let's just leave it at that.
SHARON:	No. Let's not just leave it at that. I don't know the reason. There's too much I don't understand and I want to know.
BESSIE:	I'm tired, Sharon. I'm real tired. If you want to know that bad let Laura tell you.
SHARON:	No, mother. You got to tell me. Laura's only heard it from Ray. Ray's heard it from his folks. They most likely heard it from other folk. It wouldn't be right to hear it from anybody but you. You're the only one who rightly knows and you got to tell me.
BESSIE:	How do I tell you somethin' like that? Somethin' I ain't never told nobody before, never spoke about. I hated her for what she done to your gran'father. I hated her for what she made him do to me.
SHARON:	Do to you?

Silence. BESSIE stares into space. The GIRLS watch her. Finally she turns and looks at the pots still standing on the stove.

BESSIE: All that food.

SHARON: It'll keep. *(Turning to LAURA.)* You still hungry?

LAURA shakes her head.

BESSIE: You ought to eat somethin'.

LAURA: Don't want anything.

BESSIE: Just like on that day... all that food... wasted.

SHARON: It won't be wasted, ma. It'll keep.

BESSIE: Reckon you'd best take that turkey home to Glen.

SHARON: Some maybe.

BESSIE: When you're growed up you think maybe you can forget the pain by turnin' to other things, turnin' to religion maybe, drugs... *(Pointedly)*...or reachin' out for the bottle. What do you do when you're a child an' there ain't nothin' or nobody to reach out to? Why did God make children so they could hurt so easy? At first, 'cept that she weren't here no more, it was like nothin' had really happened. Daddy went on workin' the farm just like he'd always done. Dorcus an' me went to school, came home, did our chores. There weren't that much more to do. She never did do much round the house anyway. We didn't talk about her. It was like we secretly said to ourselves not to say anything. Your grandaddy was quieter, more into hisself, but that was only natural I suppose. He'd sit out there, sometimes in the barn, or in here, and never say a word. And when you spoke to him it was like he never heard you. You had to say somethin' two, three times before he'd look at you an' the way he looked, you knew he hadn't heard, so you had to say it again. There was a difference in him though, hard to see at first, but it was there an' it was growin' all the time an' that was, sometimes, he was much more lovin', more touchin' I mean, than he'd ever been before. He'd pull me onto his lap an' stroke my hair. I had long hair then, long hair right down to my waist. He'd stroke it, run his fingers through it. He was specially lovin' with me. I was always his favorite. Maybe because I was the younger. But his touchin' got more'n more. He'd hold me round the waist, huggin', strokin' my legs. Sometimes I got a funny feelin' about it, worried by it. I would try an' slip off his lap, say I had somethin' to do or somewheres to go, homework maybe. And, when I got away, I'd go outside or up to my room an' just sit an' think. By now things were real bad for us at school. Kids kept away or called out dirty things to us and laughed among theirselves. I didn't know rightly what they was yellin' or laughin' at but it hurt, an' not havin' any friends. And I suppose it must have been the same for him. Nobody would give him the time of day and lonesomeness does strange things to a man. Anyway, one night I was asleep, and all of a sudden I woke up, and he was there, standin' next to the bed, lookin' down at me. After a while I said to him, "Daddy?" But he just said, "Shhh... there..." I was scared. I don't know why. I had this feelin' somethin' terrible was going to happen. I could feel my heart thumpin'. I could hear it. It was like it was goin' to burst. I started to cry. He sat on the bed a long time, strokin' my hair, soothin' me. I quieted down an' I remember askin' him what the trouble was, was there somethin' he wanted. How was I to know what it was he wanted? What he needed so bad? I couldn't feel his pain for him, only my own. I cried, I screamed, I cried out, "No, daddy, no! It hurts! Please, daddy, it hurts so!" I thought maybe I was bein' punished for somethin' I did. I didn't know anything. Maybe it was all my fault she treated him so bad, gone off like that an' left us. After he'd done he was cryin' again, sayin' over an' over, "My little girl... my little girl," an' how he was sorry an' how it wouldn't happen again. How he just wanted to show he loved me. After he'd gone Dorcus come to me an' asks what happened but I couldn't tell her. I didn't even know what had happened except that I had been hurt so bad. *(She takes a moment before continuing.)* I was scared of him after that. Kept away from him as much as I could. But one afternoon, when Dorcus weren't there, it happened again an' this time I told her an' she said to him she was gonna tell on him if he did it again. So he hit her. Hit her so hard near knocked her teeth loose an' said if she told anyone he'd kill her. I remember I said to Dorcus why didn't we run away. But she says, no, where would we go to anyway? I said I was sick, an' sore, an' scared, an' what was I goin' to do if he tried it again? An' she said he wouldn't do that, she'd scared him for a while an', anyway, she was gonna move in an' sleep with me, an' she did that. He didn't say anythin' about it, made out he didn't even notice. Then one day his sister drives up, gets out of the car an' you could see she was boilin' mad, looked like she was 'bout to explode. She'd been to the school an' spoke with Mrs Miller. She'd come all the way up from Lexington. Seems Dorcus wrote her an' told her bad things was happenin' an' how we needed help, an' she come up. This was your great-aunt Laura May, the one we named you after. She sent us kids outside an' when she finally called us back in the house she said we weren't stayin' here no more, she was takin' us back to live in Lexington with her an' your uncle, your great-uncle Bernard. She sent us off to pack our things. Daddy was sittin' right here, at this table, lookin' down at it, never raised his eyes. When we got back he still never looked up. When we got to the door, Dorcus turn around an' looked at him sittin' there an' she said, "I'm sorry, papa." An' then we went. We stayed in Lexington till I was big enough to look after myself an' then I come back. Daddy was a sick man by then, wasted away. Doctors couldn't help, said it maybe months, maybe years. That's why, when I married Cole, we stayed here. An' now she's dead. She, who was the cause of it all, and somehow... somehow... none of it, none of it, none of it matters.

And, finally, BESSIE breaks. She covers her face with her hands and weeps; violent, wracking sobs, uncontrollable tears.

SHARON looks at LAURA but she is sitting totally helpless, weeping in sympathy. SHARON gets up, goes to BESSIE's side, puts her arms around her.

SHARON: It's all right, mama, it's all right... Don't take on so... come on now. *(She lay's her head on her mother's.)* It's over, mama. It's all over. I think maybe you ought to lay down a spell, huh? Rest a while? Come on, let me take you.

SHARON straightens up. BESSIE removes SHARON's hand, turns to LAURA.

BESSIE: Is that how your Ray told it to you?

SHARON: Mother, don't... It's not Laura's fault. Laura never said anything to anybody.

BESSIE: *(To SHARON.)* You see why I loved your auntie Dorcus so.

SHARON: Yes, yes.

BESSIE: *(Back to LAURA.)* You see now why I got so mad with you when you run off playin' with boys like a wild thing. You see why I whipped you for it. I didn't know what to do, tryin' to keep you from losin' your childhood. The day after he came to my room, after it happened, I went down by the creek. I took the pocket book she give me and the silver bracelet, I put the bracelet inside the purse and I buried it, dug a deep hole an' buried them. That night your grandad came to my room an' locked the door was the night I lost my childhood an' I

	think I was buryin' it down there by the creek. I didn't want you to lose yours before it was time. I wanted to keep you from that and I didn't know how. I'm sorry, I didn't know how.
SHARON:	Mother, come an' lay down now, come on.
BESSIE:	Yes...Yes... *(She gets up.)* I'm tired.

SHARON takes BESSIE by the arm but BESSIE pushes her away, walks on.

	No, don't come with me. I don't want you to come with me. I'm all right.

They watch her go then SHARON turns to LAURA.

SHARON:	Jesus! How come you never told me any of this, Laura?
LAURA:	I didn't know all that stuff. Only 'bout gran'ma runnin' off with this guy an' everybody sayin' how gran'pa went a bit crazy an' his girls had to be took from him. People make up stories, all kindsa stories. It was a long time ago an' stories get all mixed up you know.
SHARON:	All these years an' she kept it to herself.
LAURA:	Who would she tell?
SHARON:	That's right. Who? Couldn't tell daddy I suppose. How would he have felt if she'd told him a thing like that? I guess he died never knowing. Makes you think, how you can live with a person year after year and not really know about them. And there was no reason for her to tell us. Funny, isn't it?
LAURA:	Funny?
SHARON:	No, I mean, there's old folks live these lives, do

	all sort of things, have all sorts of things done to them, have secrets. And if they tell you about it you got to wonder if it's true. Could all that really happen to this person who's sittin' there tellin' it to you? When you come to think of it you know, seventy, eighty years, that's a long time. You can get through a whole lot of livin' in that time.
LAURA:	Don't know as I want to live that long. Not to be like her, granm'ma, turned into a cabbage.
SHARON:	We don't know that. Don't know what was in her mind, in her thoughts. Don't know what memories she was having all the time she sat out there. What happened to her all those years she was away. Who she met, where she went, who she fell in love with, lived with. I wonder what happened to the man.
LAURA:	Guess he must've died on her. Or up an' left.
SHARON:	What makes you suppose that?
LAURA:	Why'd she come back here all poor an' shabby lookin'?
SHARON:	Guess we'll never know.
LAURA:	Guess not.
SHARON:	That is a matter for regret. Somehow I regret not knowing that.

Silence.

LAURA:	Sharon, I ain't goin' to Philadelphia.
SHARON:	What?
LAURA:	Mama was right. Comes a time you gotta stop runnin'.
SHARON:	You just gonna stay here? Marry Henry? Ray'll kill

you.

LAURA: I'll have friends.

SHARON: Oh, sure! Wrong side of the track.

LAURA: Things'll change. And I'll still have you. Won't I?

SHARON: *(Pause.)* Sure... sure...

Car headlights flash across the veranda. LAURA gets to her feet.

LAURA: Car comin'. *(She goes across to the veranda door to look out.)* You think it's Ray again?

SHARON: Not in a car. Why would he come in a car?

The dogs start up their yelping.

LAURA: I just knew he'd come back! You think he's gonna let himself be beat up by a woman an' just let it go? Not Ray. What're we gonna do?

SHARON: *(Picking up the bourbon bottle.)* We got any more of this stuff?

LAURA: SHAR-on! For Chrissakes! You gonna poison yourself with that. Quit it now, you hear? You don't need that. He could have a gun this time! He could have friends with him! He'll have been drinking, Sharon! He'll be crazy!

SHARON: Just tell him there's already been a death in the house today, that'll sober him.

LAURA: He's here. Car's stopped. It ain't Ray... It's Lindy! Oh, my God, the kids! Somethin's happened to the kids!

LAURA runs off along the veranda. BESSIE appears at the inner door.

BESSIE: There's a car. Who is it?

SHARON: Lindy Johnson.

BESSIE: Lindy? What's she want?

She goes to the veranda door to look out.

SHARON: She does happen to be lookin' after your gran'children.

BESSIE: You think somethin's happened?

SHARON: Obviously. She isn't making a social call. Lindy wouldn't be making a social call here now would she? Not the way you feel about niggers.

BESSIE: Sharon!

SHARON: Well ain't it the truth? Or should I be more polite? The way you feels about "colored folk".

BESSIE: Laura down there with her?

SHARON: Yes.

BESSIE: I ain't got nothin' 'gainst colored... blacks.

SHARON: I wonder what you would have said if one of your daughters had married one, if you had pickaninny gran'kids running around.

BESSIE: Well they didn't so what's the point of supposin'?

LAURA appears, bursts through the door and heads straight for the inner one.

What's the matter? What's happened?

LAURA: It's Henry.

LINDY appears and stands by the veranda door. She is about the same age as Sharon.

SHARON: What about Henry? Hello, Lindy.

LAURA: He's in the hospital.

She has gone into the house.

BESSIE: Where' the kids?

LINDY: At my mother's. She'll look after them. I'm sorry to hear of your sad bereavement. Laura told me. Please accept my condolences.

BESSIE nods.

I'm sorry I had to come.

BESSIE: Why did you?

SHARON: Mother! Lindy, come on in and sit down.

LINDY: Laura's just gettin' her coat an' things.

BESSIE: Where's she goin'?

SHARON: To the hospital of course.

BESSIE: Why of course?

SHARON: Sit down, Lindy. What's happend to Henry?

LINDY: He's hurt, real bad.

SHARON: How bad?

BESSIE: Why "of course"? What's he got to do with Laura?

SHARON: Mother! Will you shut up? Will you just shut up now? For God's sake! Lindy, come and sit down.

BESSIE: I want to know what's goin' on here.

SHARON: And so do I. And, if you shut up for two seconds, we'll find out. *(To LINDY.)* You look terrible.

LINDY: You don't look so hot yourself. What you been doin'?

BESSIE: Drinkin' solid all day.

SHARON: I'd offer you one. You look like you could use it, but...

LINDY: It's okay. *(Looking towards the door.)* Where is that girl?

SHARON: Have a coffee then. Make her a coffee, mama.

BESSIE gives her daughter a look and then puts a kettle on the stove to make a cup of instant.

SHARON: Now sit down and tell us what happened.

LINDY is about to sit when LAURA returns carrying a bag and coat.

LAURA: Okay, let's go.

SHARON: *(Puts a restraining hand on LINDY's arm.)* Tell us.

LAURA: We gotta go, Sharon!

SHARON: Sit down and tell us.

LINDY sits. SHARON sits.

LAURA: Sharon! There isn't time!

BESSIE: There's time. If Henry's hurt bad and lyin' in the hospital he ain't goin' nowhere in a hurry is he?

LAURA: Can't it wait?

BESSIE: (*Exploding.*) No! You wait, dammit!

Then she carries on with her coffee making. LAURA stands. SHARON waits for LINDY to talk which she eventually does. She is quiet, matter of fact.

LINDY: I needed some stuff for dinner, some things I run out of, forgot to get. So I asks Henry if he don' mind takin' a ride down to the 7 Eleven. He says "Sure." He's watchin' the game on tv but he gets up, gets his hat, an' goes out. An' that's the last time I sees him till I see him lyin' there in the hospital.

SHARON: An accident? Car crash?

LINDY: The police come to the house to tell me. Didn't use their siren. Didn't use their lights. I'm in the middle of cookin' an' there comes this knock on the door. Lucius says, "I'll get it, ma". He opens the door an' there's this policeman standin' there. I was wipin' my hands. I could have died of fright. You know? I goes all cold an' there's this terrible feelin' in my stomach an' I feel like I can't breathe. But I hears what he's sayin' an' I know somethin' terrible's happened. He says, "Good-evenin' ma'am". Then I see there's two of 'em. They's very nice, very polite, sayin' as to how they was sorry an' they'd drive me. An' I said, would they take me to my mother's first so I could leave the kids there with her. An' they look around an' see six scared kids starin' at 'em, an' Francine starts to cry so they radio for another car. Well, pretty soon it come, an' we take the kids to my mother's an' then I goes on down to the hospital. (*She stops for a moment.*) An' they say I can see Henry if I wants but it ain't pretty, an' not to expect him to say nothin' seein' how he's still unconscious and they're worried he's in a real bad way. So I sees him. An' the doctor says to me, in a whisper like, you know, he says they just gotta wait till he comes 'round. They won't know the full extent of the damage till then. Sounds like he's talkin' about some broken down old engine or somethin'. An' all the time I'm lookin' at Henry's mashed up face. Thank you.

BESSIE has placed the cup of coffee in front of her. LINDY picks up the cup but, an inch off the table, her nerveless fingers let it go. She is now trembling violently.

Oh, my God! I'm sorry, I'm sorry!

There is confusion as three people rush to the rescue, all talking at once. LAURA grabs LINDY's shoulders. BESSIE dabs frantically at the spilled coffee. SHARON rescues the cup and also tries cleaning up.

LAURA: Lindy!

BESSIE: Did you burn yourself? Are you all right?

SHARON: It's okay, Lindy, it's okay.

LAURA: It's shock! It's shock! What're we do?

SHARON: Lindy! Lindy!

LINDY is now weeping. She has folded her arms across her chest and is rocking back and forth. Out of the chaos comes her voice, almost a scream of pain.

LINDY: Why? Why did they do it? He never done nothin' to them. Henry never hurt no one in his whole life.

There is a shocked silence. LINDY is still rocking. SHARON sits down beside her and they wait. In the silence BESSIE takes the cup to the sink and she stays there.

If I'd remembered to get those things... *(One trembling hand flutters to her mouth.)*... If he'd said he just wanted to finish watchin' the game...

SHARON puts out her hand, takes LINDY's. LINDY turns to her.

SHARON: Don't, Lindy... Don't... It's no good trying to lay blame, saying, "If... if this... if that". Won't do any good.

LINDY: Seems like he come out of the 7 Eleven with the stuff, goes to the car... Mrs Wainwright's sittin' in her car, 'bout to drive off, an' this is how she told it to the police... He goes to the car an' this voice yells out, "Hey, nigger!" Well, Henry pays no mind. Someone calls him nigger he never takes no notice. he ain't the fightin' kind. I never seen him get riled up, ever, not even when we was kids. He don't like trouble. Would sooner walk away. It ain't that he's scared. I seen him once stop a Dobermann dog was about killin' a small one. Got hisself bit in the hand but he pulled that Dobermann off an' he held it till its owner come runnin up. Anyway, he opens the car door an' that's as far as he get. They pull him back an' turn him around and it's Ray an' his friends, four of 'em altogether. An' Ray says somethin' like, "Hey, nigger, I hear you're gonna be new daddy to my kids. Well, we'll see 'bout that." An' they beat him up. Kicked him. Kicked him all the while he was layin' on the ground. Nobody come to help. Folks in the store just stand an' watch through the window, through the doors. Just stood there, starin'. Mrs Wainwright's too scared to get out of her car. When they get tired of kickin' him they all pile into Hank Lattimore's truck an' drive off. Then the police come, ambulance, an' they take him to the hospital.

SHARON: You stupid bitch, Laura! I thought you said nobody knows. You said...

It is now LINDY's turn to lay a restraining hand on SHARON's arm.

LINDY: No, Sharon, don't lay blame. That's what you told me. Henry knowed what he was doin'. It ain't Laura's fault. Don't blame her.

SHARON: Have they caught them?

LINDY: They got Hank an' the other two. But they ain't found Ray yet. Last I heard the police was out lookin' for him.

LAURA: I'm goin' to the hospital now... Lindy?

LINDY: Yes, yes, I'm comin'.

She gets up. LAURA has moved to the door and is holding it open.

I'm sorry.

She goes to LAURA and they go out. BESSIE has not moved from the sink. SHARON sits down again. Silence.

BESSIE: So that's what Philadelphia was all about.

SHARON: Pity they didn't go sooner.

BESSIE rinses out the cup, puts it on the drainer, crosses the room to go back into the house. SHARON watches until she is almost at the door.

You're glad.

BESSIE: Glad?

SHARON: Pleased it happened. You're pleased.

BESSIE: I'm sorry Henry Johnson's been hurt.

SHARON: Your shithead son-in-law and his friends who haven't got the brains of a cockroach between them near kick a man to death and you're pleased.

BESSIE: I don't see how you can say that, Sharon. I said I was sorry.

SHARON: Sorry, my ass! And you're the one talking about

	hurt, talking about pain, talking about kindness, and gentleness. And here's a gentle man, a kind man, a lovin' man, and all you can think of is you most likely won't have to face having him for a son-in-law. You won't have to face the shame you think it is. You think there's been too much talk about this family already so let's not have anymore. Well let me tell you, Henry Johnson's ten times the man Ray Peterson or any of those others will ever be and, if he was to marry Laura, she wouldn't want for better. I'm not so sure about the other way round but that is Henry Johnson's business. You should be proud he wants your daughter. You should be fucking proud.
BESSIE:	I'm sorry he's been hurt. I'm real sorry.
SHARON:	Is that all you can say? Oh, go to bed. There's no point in even talking to you. I'm talking to your mother here, your father, your grandparents, and their parents before them. I'm talking to generations here. I don't want to talk anymore. I don't want to even try. Go to bed.

Pause.

BESSIE:	You gonna sit there all night?
SHARON:	What I do is my business. What Laura does is her business. What her kids do is their business. What you do is your business. Stop asking. We talk about loving people but we don't. All the time we're asking things of them. We can't say, "I love you", without asking, "Do you love me?" We talk about loving God but we don't. All the time we're asking things of Him. If you hadn't asked so much of Laura when she was a kid maybe she would never have married that bastard in the first place. If you hadn't asked so much of her she would have told you about Henry and you would have given instead of asking. You would have given him to her and her to him and been glad for them because you truly

loved her. You wouldn't have asked, "Is it right? Is it wrong? What will folk think? What will they say? What will happen? Where do I stand?" It's her life. Well there's got to come a time when we stop asking because, most of the time, what we're asking for is the impossible. I'm sorry, mama, I'm not sure what I'm saying here. I'm drunk. Well and truly drunk. Go to bed.

BESSIE crosses back to the sink to get a glass of water. There is the sound of a motor bike in the distance. The sound gets louder. BESSIE looks out of the window.

The light from the bike's headlamp flashes across the veranda and into the room, and again, and again, one way then the other as the bike roars around the yard. The dogs bark furiously.

SHARON gets up, crosses to the corner, picks up the shotgun. But, before she can make the door, BESSIE stops her, holds out her hands. There is a long moment and then SHARON hands over the gun.

BESSIE: Godammit!

She goes out onto the veranda. The sound of the motor bike is almost deafening.

BLACKOUT.

Song page 27

Author's Note: Bessie's Monologues pages 69-72 and 74-77

Although this speech might seem to be inordinately long, it has been shown in productions in the USA [James Madison University, Virginia and Carnegie Mellon University Pittsburgh] to completely hold audience attention, especially if blocked with no movement and no distraction. The three women should remain at the table with all concentration on Bessie.

Movement or business of any kind (Smoking, drinking) distracts from the power of Bessie's Story.

www.ingramcontent.com/pod-product-compliance
Lightning Source LLC
Chambersburg PA
CBHW020016050426

42450CB00005B/497